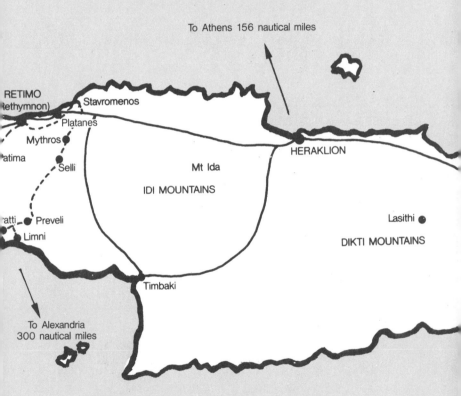

AEGEAN SEA

To Athens 156 nautical miles

RETIMO
(Rethymnon)
Stavromenos
Platanes
Mythros
atima
Selli
Mt Ida
IDI MOUNTAINS
HERAKLION
ratti   Preveli
Limni
Lasithi
DIKTI MOUNTAINS
Timbaki
To Alexandria
300 nautical miles

MEDITERRANEAN SEA

Flowers of Rethymnon

German parachutists landing near Suda Bay on 20 May 1941. A Junkers 52 crashing in the centre.

Flowers of Rethymnon

ESCAPE FROM CRETE

Lew Lind

Kangaroo Press

N.B. Throughout the text English spelling, as used on British Army maps during World War II, is used for the principal place names. i.e. Athens (Athene), Canea (Hania), Heraklion (Iraklion), Retimo (Rethymnon), and Sfakia (Chora Sfakion).

Jacket: Vernon Jones
The battle of Retimo, 1972
Oil on canvas 152.5 × 244 cm
Australian War Memorial (27776)

This edition first published in 1991 by Kangaroo Press Pty Ltd
3 Whitehall Road (P.O. Box 75) Kenthurst 2156
Typeset by G.T. Setters Pty Limited
Printed by Southwood Press Pty Ltd, Marrickville 2204

ISBN 0 86417 394 6

CONTENTS

INTRODUCTION

This book is a new edition of *Escape From Crete*, which has become a collector's item in the half century since I wrote it in 1944. World War II was still in progress then and Crete was still under the iron heel of German occupation. Of necessity, the original manuscript was heavily censored by the Admiralty to protect those courageous Cretans who had risked their lives to assist escaped prisoners of war like me to evade recapture. Consequently, the names of people, villages and towns, service units and other information considered of use to the enemy were deleted. Likewise, three incidents which appeared in the original manuscript were replaced by alternative copy.

In this edition I have reintroduced this information by the use of endnotes and this has resulted in a more readable and historically correct narrative. I have also included, as an appendix, the text of an address on the Cretan campaign that I delivered to the Naval Historical Society of Australia in 1971. This address puts my experiences in a wider historical and military context.

Escape From Crete was selected by John Laird, Associate Professor of English in the Faculty of Military Studies at the University of New South Wales, as an example of memorable war literature by Australian writers in his fine anthology, *The Australian Experience of War*.

Finally, the title of this edition has been changed to *Flowers of Rethymnon* which alludes to the Cretan belief that symbolically, the spirits of the Australian soldiers who died in the battle are immortalised in the flowers that grow at Rethymnon.

I was nineteen years of age when the events described in this book took place. On the day war was declared I was called up with my Militia unit to guard vital oil fuel installations in the Sydney area and seven weeks later, when recruiting commenced for the Second Australian Imperial Force, I enlisted at Marrickville Army Barracks. Having opted for artillery, I was posted to the 2/3rd Field Regiment. The first all-state unit raised for the AIF, it consisted of men from all states of the Commonwealth and not a few from New Guinea and other areas outside Australia.

We sailed to war on a wave of youthful euphoria in the world's largest troopship, the former Trans-Atlantic liner *Queen Mary*. Three weeks out from Australia the growing concern of Italy entering the war on the side of Germany caused our Middle East-bound convoy to be diverted to Cape Town and from there to Great Britain. We arrived as the British Expeditionary Force was returning from Dunkirk.

My regiment moved into a camp at Tidworth on the Salisbury Plains, a few miles north of the fine country residence Admiral Nelson bought for Lady Hamilton. For some weeks we trained as infantry for our role in resisting a possible German invasion of southern England, but in late August we were issued with the first 25-pounder field guns manufactured. The gunners and specialists of the regiment attended a course at Britain's famous 'university of artillery' at Larkhill—we were the only Australian artillery regiment to be so honoured.

The Battle of Britain commenced in the second week of September and we had a box seat, the flight path from France to London passed over our camp. On their inward flight the German aerial armadas flew at a great height, but often on their return they hedgehopped over the fields. The first enemy fire directed by an enemy at my regiment was delivered one morning by one of these low-flying aircraft.

We sailed from England in November, just as the weather turned cold. Six weeks later, on New Year's Day, 1941, we arrived in Egypt. Within two weeks of our arrival one of our batteries was committed in the Libyan Campaign. It distinguished itself in the capture of Tobruk and a few days later gained further laurels at Benghasi.

In the first days of March we were warned for embarkation to Greece. We landed at the port of Piraeus on 2 April and seven days later we were dug in at the entrance to Kolide Pass, a few miles south of the village of Vevi. The Yugoslav border was to the north. It snowed lightly on 10 April and the German

advance guard crossed the border. They advanced a little over
a mile and the regiment engaged them with well-directed fire.

Like most soldiers in battle, we knew little of the overall
operations. Even at the time we were engaging the advance
guard of the Adolph Hitler Armoured Division the New Zealand
Division on our flank was withdrawing. The snow fell more
heavily and by the morning of 11 April we were fighting in snow
up to our waists. It was bitterly cold, and we were still wearing
the uniforms we wore in the desert.

The battle at Vevi lasted three days and the range fell from
13,000 yards to 200 yards, with the German infantry on the road
which led south. We extricated ourselves from the snow drifts
and fell back to a temporary holding point on Lake Petron.

In all, my regiment fought six battles in Greece: Vevi, Lake
Petron, Servia, Ellason, Kriekuri and Markopoloun. These were
rearguard actions protecting the retreating British and Greek
armies. In every case, the guns remained in action until the
infantry had disengaged and withdrawn through our gun
positions. At Ellason, the twenty-one guns of the regiment—
we had lost two in the withdrawal from Vevi and a third had
crashed into a gorge as we withdrew from Servia—fired a record
6,500 rounds in a continuous twelve-hour shoot. The Official
History records we severely mauled the tanks and armoured
vehicles of the German 2nd and 9th Armoured Divisions. This
was a remarkable achievement for an understrength regiment
and we were justly proud. We supported the New Zealand 4th
Brigade in the battles at Kriekuri and Markopoloun. The latter
was a day-long battle fought in the open under continuous enemy
air attack, but the line held. We fought with our backs to the
sea, holding the beaches of Porto Rafti from which we were to
be evacuated.

Our last action in Greece was fought a bare 100 yards from
the beach. We held the line until midnight and then spirited
away in the dark to be ferried out to the light cruiser HMS *Ajax*
which carried us to Crete. We left behind us the self-destructed
25-pounder guns which had served us so well.

The island of Crete rose out of the sea like a gigantic monster, its peaks rising range after range out of the early morning mist. From the crowded deck of the cruiser it frowned down upon us like an evil ogre. Spontaneously, we named it the Isle of Doom.

Of all the battles of World War II none made a more lasting impression on those who participated in it than the Battle of Crete. Half a century later I remember vividly the cauldron of fire and explosion. I have forgotten neither the battle nor the months which followed it. When the war ended I initiated through my regimental association a Clothing for Crete Appeal. Hundreds of garments for all ages and an equal number of shoes and accessories were collected, dry-cleaned and packed carefully into a large crate. Funds were raised by raffles and donations to meet the cost of shipment and distribution. I enlisted the assistance of the British Consul for Canea, Mr Edgar Vidova, to supervise the delivery of the parcels to the many villages in the highland areas of western and central Crete.

Despite the assurances of the shipping company, the crate was lost for several months at the transhipment port of Genoa. Further funds were raised to pay the additional wharfage accrued. Twelve months after the crate sailed from Sydney I received a letter from Mr Vidova advising that the parcels had been delivered to the villages. However, many years later I learnt the truck carrying the gifts had plunged into a gorge and many parcels were stolen from the wreckage. One, fortunately, did arrive at the village of Zebrou in the depths of the bitter winter of 1947 when the small community was snowbound and in danger of freezing to death. In late 1941 this village had been burnt by the Germans for sheltering another Australian and myself.

I maintained a close relationship with the Cretan people over the years which followed and have returned to the island on five occasions to renew the bond. In Australia I have also been closely associated with the Cretans who migrated in the years after World War II.

In 1985 I returned to Crete for the filming of the full-length docu-dramatisation of *Flowers of Rethymnon*. I narrated the film in situ in the high mountain villages and my part as a nineteen-year-old soldier was played by Australian actor Mark Owen Taylor. The film has been screened in Australia, New Zealand, Greece, Germany and Great Britain.

Five years later I accompanied an Australian production team from Channel 9's 'Sixty Minutes' program to make a documentary for the fiftieth anniversary of the Crete Campaign.

I, and others who shared similar experiences, know there is no escape from Crete for those who have fallen under the spell of the mountain heart of the island and the hearts of the people who live there. Like Lord Byron and Patrick Leigh Fermor, I know Cretan bonds are forever.

Lew Lind, March 1991

KISAMO BAY

CANEA BAY

KAMPOS

MALEME

C. KRIO

PALAIOKHORO

CANEA

GALATOS

SUDA BAY

KALEVIS

SPHAKIA

GEORGIOPOUS

RETIMO

HAGIA TRIADA

C. LITTINOS

MEDITERRANEAN   SEA

The flowers of Rethymnon grow taller
in those places where Australian
soldiers died in the Battle of Crete.
Their blood is mingled with the sacred
soil of Crete. These quiet places have never
been ploughed and never will be ploughed.
They are sacred to all Cretans forever.

Aristedes Lioniatakis,
Battle of Crete Celebrations, 1975

2/3 rd. FIELD REGIMENT

1

ISLE OF DOOM

The old *Ajax* had been making good time.[1] Once or twice she had touched thirty knots, so they told us, but we were too weary to be excited by mere bursts of speed. Dirty and bearded, we sprawled in untidy heaps about the deck watching the outline of the coast looming mistily in the early morning light. There were no rations aboard but those of us who were lucky munched at bully beef and biscuits.

Word had been passed that we were not bound for Alexandria after all, but for Crete, where we were to await more adequate transport.

Two hours later the ship had glided between two headlands

The light cruiser HMS *Ajax*, which evacuated the 2/3rd Field Regiment from Greece.

and through an opening in the anti-submarine net protecting Suda Bay, which was crowded with all types of craft from cruisers to invasion barges. Several transports were unloading against a background of rugged mountains rising step by step from a narrow strip of plain. To our tired eyes the landscape was green and restful.

Landing barges were soon alongside and, tumbling down the ladders into them, we were whisked to a wharf. The air-raid sirens sounded as we scrambled ashore, but nobody heeded them. Work everywhere went on without interruption. Near us, a destroyer which had apparently been hit by a bomb astern, was moored. Sailors were cleaning up a gory mess and helping wounded shipmates ashore.

Once on the road we were split into two parties in obedience to a printed notice enjoining: 'Australians Left—New Zealand and British Forces Right'. The route taken by the Australians seemed to lead on for ever. Hour after hour we trudged in the heat, often on the edge of towering cliffs. 'How much further?' we would ask of those who passed. 'Just up the road,' they would reply. One of the lads, sweating like the rest of us and viewing the rough and hilly terrain with the disfavour we all shared christened the land 'The Isle of Doom'.[2] How right he was!

Our bivouac was on the banks of a lovely, fast-flowing stream fed by the snow on white-capped peaks. The water was marvellously clear and refreshing. Food, however, was still a problem. Those of us who had money accordingly made our way to Kalevis, a village about a quarter of a mile distant, to buy what we could. We bought bread at fifteen drachmas a loaf but supplies were quickly exhausted for some of our men had thousands of drachma! It was not surprising to see two of our infantry boys and a group of Greeks playing at two-up in the main street.

An order had been received at Regimental Headquarters that we were to be formed into three companies of infantry and to be trained as such. In the morning the regiment was paraded, detailed to various companies and marched to the QM dump to be issued with grease-spattered Springfield rifles and fifty rounds of ammunition a man. Each company was informed of the sector of the beach it would have to defend and was marched to its allotted area. At two o'clock in the afternoon there was an air alert. Within fifteen minutes a formation of about thirty German bombers roared overhead. Though the AA guns put up a continuous barrage over the harbour the Jerries dived through it and released their loads. Four Gloster-Gladiator fighters intercepted and the fighting moved out to sea beyond our sight.

During the next four days we concentrated on our training. We were a motley crowd still dressed in the clothes in which we had escaped from Greece. In singlet and trousers, with a bandolier of cartridges over our shoulders, and rifles slung with rope, we marched miles and miles over hill and down dale, sweating and grouching. We were 'toughening up' in earnest. As nothing more had been heard about going on to Alexandria we resigned ourselves to our fate.

Then, on the eighth day after coming to Suda Bay, we found ourselves in an olive clearing lending attentive ear to the GOC, Major-General Freyberg, who warned us of the imminence of an airborne invasion and did not fail to stress the inadequacy of our strength to defend the island.

Philosophically, a few of my mates and I decided to spend the afternoon in Canea, where, an hour afterwards, an ancient Greek bus deposited us in the main street. It was market day but there were pathetically few goods for sale. The town itself, however, was picturesque. Flat-roofed buildings of two storeys, packed side by side, faced one another placidly across narrow cobbled streets and alleys which sloped down to the waterfront.

We learned next morning that fresh orders had been given that the infantry companies were to be disbanded and that artillery troops were to be formed to take up positions at different points. The few who remained of our old troop constituted the nucleus of one of these new troops. Most of our old officers were with us.

Early next day we packed our meagre gear and moved to Suda Bay where, having completed a three-hour march, we halted at an ordnance dump just off 'Forty-second Street'. A battalion of Royal Marines, newly landed from a transport, was settling into camp close by. Compared with the hardened, though tattered, Aussie and Kiwi contingents these fellows seemed very raw and clean, their immaculate equipment and kitbags making them look incongruous.

Some of the guns from the *York*[3], which had been sunk in the harbour and was sitting comfortably on the bottom with her deck just above water, had been dismantled and reassembled ashore.[3] They were to be manned by the marines.

We collected our own guns—Italian 105 mm pieces captured in Libya.[4] It was no light task to manhandle them across the beach and aboard an invasion barge.[5] By the time we had done this and loaded ammunition and stores, darkness was upon us. Yet, when our captain suggested a concert we thought it a bright idea. Having persuaded the crew of the barge to act the part of audience we gave what we—and even the audience—considered to be a good show.

One of the two former Italian guns used by the author at Retimo.

As we had orders not to proceed until dusk next day, we had nearly twenty-four hours to while away. After spending a quiet night we investigated the mechanism of the barge, which was still on the secret list. Except for a raid alarm at 11 a.m. the time passed uneventfully. At 7 p.m. the barge pulled out and headed east along the coast for Retimo (Rethymnon), where we grounded shortly before midnight. Although enemy planes were overhead and flares were dropping no more than a mile from us we at once began unloading, helped by a party of infantrymen. The job was quickly finished and the barge then slipped away in the darkness, leaving us to our own resources.

There was little or no leisure during the ensuing few days which were occupied in digging our two guns into pits, camouflaging them and preparing our defences for the assault that was expected at any hour. The guns were in the corners of a wheat field on the side of a hill overlooking the aerodrome. At thirty yards distance they were invisible—a feat of camouflage of which we were very proud. Lacking camouflage nets we had requisitioned fishing nets in the town and woven them with wheat stalks.

Rations, as usual, were very short, but we were able to buy food from neighbouring Cretans who, without exception, went out of their way to be friendly and helpful. Cigarettes and tobacco, of course, existed only in memory. Some of the more enterprising among us cultivated the art of 'bumper-shooting' or experimented with tea leaves and various grasses without noticeable enjoyment.

It was on 18 May—incidentally, our eighteenth day on the island—that the Germans began to be really aggressive. They bombed Retimo thoroughly for half an hour. As the aerodrome was a dispersal 'drome and the fighters used it only at dusk and dawn the Germans were able to attack without interception. Originally there had been nine Gloster-Gladiators using the field but each day one or more had failed to return.[6] On this particular morning only five had taken off.

All next morning enemy strafing continued, with Retimo as the main target. The town was alight in many places and the local olive-oil factory blazed like an orange flare. Over the whole area hung a heavy pall of smoke, and in the distance we could hear bombs exploding at Suda Bay. Inhabitants, with pathetic bundles under their arms, were streaming to the hills.

In a little time Jerry diverted his attention from Retimo and commenced systematically to bomb and strafe our infantry defences. One of his planes, a Dornier, was hit and crash-landed on the opposite side of the airfield. Overhead, two gallant Gloster-Gladiators attacked a formation of about twenty bombers. They never had a chance, but it was an inspiring fight which held us enthralled. Twisting and squirming, the British planes, at odds of ten to one, tried to drive the formation out to sea. One of the bombers fell like a wounded bird, to be quickly followed into the water by a Gloster-Gladiator, in flames. Three Dorniers were on the tail of the other lone fighter and the battle was over in a few seconds. The British plane, blazing like a torch, fell into a crazy spin and dived headlong into the sea.

The Dornier forced down on the aerodrome was found to contain accurate maps of our areas and some of our defensive positions were neatly spotted.[7] This meant, naturally, that we had to dig new pits in other places without waste of a moment. Nevertheless, we were allowed to pause from our labours at 8 p.m. to hear a message from Mr Churchill read—a message in which we were told that the following day would bring our greatest trial and that we had the best wishes of the Government.

At four o'clock in the morning we stood-to, and by daylight enemy medium bombers and fighters began to bomb, dive-bomb and machine-gun our positions, as well as the town. This force had no sooner withdrawn than we saw a mass of aircraft in very close formation approaching low over the sea from the north. As they drew near they increased their elevation and began to circle. At first glance they appeared to be heavy bombers and fighters, but our Captain, on taking a look through his binoculars, passed the word that they were troop-carriers towing gliders. We made ready for whatever might happen, but the formation passed on to the west.

Word came that paratroops and troop-carrying gliders had

German paratroopers advancing along a gully after landing in Crete on 20 May.

landed at the Maleme airfield and that some of the paratroops
were believed to be wearing New Zealand uniforms.

Meanwhile, the attack, both by bombing and machine-gun
strafing, continued all around us, chiefly against our infantry.
We knew we would not have long to wait. Indeed, our worst
fears were confirmed when at three in the afternoon a cloud
of planes was seen flying low towards us from the north-west.
On approaching they proved to be three-engined Junkers. Once
over the beach they circled, and came at us from the east,
levelling out at a height of about 150 feet.

Things began to happen.

Hundreds of dark figures burst from the sides of the planes,
dropped for a second like plummets, and then bloomed into
colour. They were paratroops, and the sky seemed to be full
of them. Green, brown, white, blue, yellow and red parachutes
fell like confetti, and already our troops on the eastern perimeter
of the 'drome were firing at them with rifles and Brens.

All the Jerries came to earth, dead or alive, on the eastern
side. Our own infantry, however, had been given strict orders
to conserve ammunition and held their fire, but we could hear
the uproar of battle in a spot obscured by thick groves of olives.

Within half an hour a fresh formation of aircraft was observed
coming in from the sea. Every man's eyes were focused upon
it, for it was realised, by now, what this portended.

Circling once, the planes straightened up and roared over the
airfield until they were almost above us, where they became the
target of a hail of small-arms fire from B Battalion.[8] Doors
sprang open, olive-clad figures were silhouetted for a moment
or two, and then they began to jump. Hit in a vital spot, the
leading Junkers slipped clumsily into a dive and crashed into
a clump of trees 200 yards in our rear. There was an explosion
and a great pillar of flame.

Overhead, billowing parachutes had nearly blotted out the
sky. Hanging from them were weird shapes clad in crash helmets
and overalls. Their knees were hunched up close to their chins
and they were firing Tommy guns clamped between their knees.
They seemed to be landing everywhere and some floated past
not more than ten feet above our heads.[9] Many had been hit

and their bodies, on striking the ground, gave a flip like a clasp-knife. Three, whose parachutes had not opened, crashed with crunchy thuds. The firing was so intense that we lay in the bottom of our gun pits. Mingling with the shouting of orders were the cries of the wounded, the crack of rifle fire, the thuds of grenades and the rattling coughs of machine-guns and Tommy guns.

A hundred yards down the hill the Germans tried to storm A Company's lines but found the defenders too much for them. Farther down the slope C Company put up a terrific fire. What had happened to B Company we could not see, for it was on the other side of the hill. Captain ——[10] crawled over and told us to remain where we were until further orders. Germans were everywhere and their snipers were taking a good count.

The sky seemed to be heavy with planes bombing and machine-gunning our troops on the flat. Another mass of troop-carriers, too, had dropped men in Retimo, but we were too busy to worry about that. Just then a section from C Company was seen crawling past us, about ten yards away. Snipers caught them in the open and two of the lads were hit. The German fire seemed to come from a large olive grove. The corporal of the section rose to his feet and ran towards a tree. He got the sniper, all right, bayonetting him from the ground with an upward thrust. The body fell to the ground squirming.

Another batch of aircraft was releasing its load overhead. This time, the cargo wasn't paratroops, but supplies. When two containers lodged within a few yards of our pit they were promptly dragged in. Upon opening them, we had a pleasant surprise. Instead of ammunition we found in each a four-gallon thermos of coffee and eight dozen hot cakes!

We were ordered to engage a number of transport planes crash-landing on the beach. Our guns, however, were very inaccurate, their sights being useless. We aimed by looking down the barrels, loaded, cocked the muzzles up, and prayed they wouldn't blow up as we fired. Bullets sang over our heads and we were far from comfortable. 'B' sub gun scored a direct hit on a Junker, which burst into a sheet of flame. The Germans, however, had been unloading small field guns and ammunition for about twenty minutes and were making good use of Verey lights to signal their aircraft. Unfortunately, too, the other planes had been landed on dead ground and we were unable to engage them.

We were ordered to form a circle around the guns throughout the night to frustrate any enemy attempt to rush them. Straws were drawn to select the man who would have the rifle.[11] The rest of us armed ourselves with shovels and pick-handles! Some prisoners were brought in by the infantrymen and we helped to search them. Generally, the paratroops were young fellows, and many wore decorations. Captain ———[12] brought in a rather unwilling captive—a colonel of true Prussian type, bull-necked and close-cropped.[13] He swore copiously in German and the persuasion of a bayonet was necessary to keep him in motion. He was a completely nasty specimen.

The night passed slowly, spasmodic bursts of fire, the occasional crump of a grenade and the moans and outcries of wounded keeping our nerves on edge. No word had come from ———[14] Battalion on the other side of the aerodrome, but the sound of firing from that direction indicated that heavy fighting was still going on.

At the first streak of dawn the infantry began to mop up the enemy positions on the side of the hill, and, undeterred by strong opposition, closed in with their bayonets. A steady line of prisoners was led back to our lines. The operation was necessarily limited because of the activity of the German bombers and dive-bombers, which were plastering every target within sight.

During the night the Jerries had erected a field hospital at the side of the road,[15] half-way between their own lines and ours. The sides were liberally draped with Red Cross flags and on the roof was a Swastika. In clear view a doctor and two orderlies gathered up the wounded, taking advantage of a lull in ground activity to perform this work of mercy. Later in the morning contact was regained with the battalion on the eastern edge of the airfield, where, we learned, casualties had been severe on both sides, particularly among our artillerymen. German paratroops had alighted in the gun pits and shot the unarmed crews at their posts. Many men who had had no weapons had by now, however, equipped themselves with rifles, pistols, Tommy guns and machine-guns captured from the invaders, some of whom had been forced back into the village by B and C companies.

Towards evening a German float-plane came down on our side of Retimo and taxied impudently inshore, where we immediately opened fire upon it with our field gun. When we saw a rubber boat put off with a radio of some kind in it we made that our target. Going wide, one of our shells struck the plane, instantly setting it ablaze. Afterwards, word came through that the ——[16] Battalion had cleared its area and bottled up most of the Germans in the ruined olive-oil factory.

That, roughly, was the situation at ten o'clock next morning when the enemy began to pound us with his field-pieces from a spot about 1,500 yards in front. We returned the fire, but as our camouflage had been destroyed and the Germans had good gun-sights the luck with not with us. Our shells fell very close to his battery but, on the other hand, his were landing very near to us, and he was firing two rounds, to our one.

The gun I was helping to serve was ordered to cease firing, but Sergeant ——'s[17] gun remained in action, momentarily hidden by the dust of a German shell that had burst fifty yards short. The crew had let one more round go when there came a short, sharp shriek as the next enemy projectile scored a direct hit on their gun. We sprang out of our pit and ran across. Peering through the blinding dirt and dust we saw six mutilated forms lying round the shattered gun. Our cobbers, the laughing, joking men we had eaten breakfast with only a little while before, were just so many bloody messes. Ted, groaning in his death agony, still clutched the tail of the gun; Jack lay dismembered near the breach he had so patiently cleaned—and the others...

Red-hot tears welled in our eyes as we desperately tried to help those who still had life in them. Shells bursting around us were unheeded. Two, including the Sergeant, were breathing.

They were quickly placed on stretchers and carried towards our casualty clearing station, the Sergeant, as he was taken away, breaking faintly into his favourite song, 'Adieu'.

Fifty yards along the track the man at the front of one of the stretchers fell to the ground with a sniper's bullet through his brain. He had been the only occupant of the gun pit who had not been hit by the shell. The two on the stretchers died before nightfall.

With the remaining gun we re-opened fire on the enemy position, and their reply was immediate and hot, the first two shells lobbing only five yards in front of our pit. Lieutenant ——[18] ordered us off the gun and we were just able to leap clear as the third enemy shell lodged clean in the pit.

On instructions three of us reported to C Company's head-quarters for special duty. We were to be taken out by a Bren-carrier to retrieve a German two-pounder which had been dropped by five parachutes from a plane. The gun was reported to be in perfect condition and obviously would be very useful.

Climbing into the carrier we were soon speeding, revolvers in hand, towards the enemy-held village and past darkened houses.[19] Swinging down the road between the opposing lines we eventually located the gun and brought it back without incident. We took it with us when we moved forward with C Company at dawn to occupy a position in the village. The company met with no resistance and we were able to place the gun in a spot from which it would be possible to fire around two houses. A farm cart was wheeled in front of it as a camouflage. Except for mortar fire, the infantry was not seriously opposed and, by 6 a.m., had reached the village bridge.[20]

Meanwhile, a force of Greek paramilitary police cadets from the Academy at Retimo, essaying an outflanking move, isolated the strong German position in the Church of St George on the high ground to the south of Perivolia. Our guns on Hill B were bringing fire down on the church, whose tall steeple was pierced with three windows through which machine-guns swept the open ground our troops had to cross. We were ordered to try and destroy the enemy posts.

We opened fire at a range of 1,500 yards and soon ranged on the target. The first two rounds blew out the top window, the third knocked out another and the fourth and fifth blew out the last one and brought the steeple crashing down in a cloud of dust.[21]

About 8 a.m. we received a report that the target was destroyed. The Greek cadets captured the church, but while they followed the retreating survivors another German company re-occupied it.

We felt that we were one up on the Jerries for what they had done to our lads the day before. Nor had we long to wait for further good shooting. A Jerry mortar was spotted firing from the sand-bagged doorway of a farmer's cottage some 800 yards away on our left front. It was a beautiful target, and before the Germans had realised what was happening we plumped four or five HEs among them. One of them, in the act of running for more tenable cover, was cut down by a Bren.

We were resting on our laurels at noon when a formation of troop-carrying planes swung in from the sea and circled overhead as though preparing to drop paratroops. Instead, they dropped stores along the bitumen road within the German lines. We were ordered to blow up the stores, if possible, or to prevent the enemy from securing them. In due course a party of Germans emerged. Two of our shells fell square into the middle of a group and left five sprawling in the road. The others spurted for cover. Retaliatory bullets from a sniper's rifle sang over our heads. We laughed to hear them.

2

BEGINNING OF THE END

Within a very short while, however, our optimism evaporated. It was plain to all of us that the Germans were bent upon blitzing the village with the object of making it untenable.

First came dive-bombers and Messerschmitt 110s whose attentions drove us headlong into the dubious shelter of a stone shack. All around the ground heaved under the concussion of exploding bombs and, even worse, we were subjected to a low-level strafing which set up a nerve-racking din.

It did not take long to reduce the village to a smoking ruin. When our shack was set on fire, we had the option of being roasted alive or of running the gauntlet for the cover of an olive grove 200 yards away. I dashed through the smoke into the open but had run only a short distance when, with a scream, a plane dived down and flattened me to the ground. The rush of air from the machine almost lifted me up again and the area all round me was peppered with cannon-shot. Twice more, before I could get to those trees the plane dived and attacked; one of its bullets splitting the German rifle in my hands. It was quite a time before I could recover my breath and calm down.

Under cover of darkness we moved our gun to a vineyard on the opposite side of the road and did our best to camouflage it. Our casualties had been heavy and all the companies of ——[1] Battalion were below strength. The enemy, however, had suffered even more severely, for next day, on one side alone of the hill facing the sea, we could count 400 of their dead. The stench from these bodies was sickening.

Most of our own dead had been buried during the night beside the little casualty clearing station which had been established in a clearing among the trees. Many of our wounded had died for lack of medical supplies, the shortage being so acute that until anaesthetics could be captured from the enemy amputations had to be performed without them. One doctor was trying to cope with two or three hundred wounded, all of whom were lying in the open. In many cases the bandages and dressings were strips torn from silken parachutes.[2]

In the afternoon we spotted a bunch of Germans drawing water from a well just behind our lines. They presented a most satisfactory target and we quickly scattered them with direct hits on the well and scaffolding.

Although there was little activity on the ground, the Luftwaffe, as usual, continued periodically to blot out the sky. Nevertheless, a good deal of the strafing was ineffective and apparently aimless.

Fresh bursts of fire were heard from eastward of the aerodrome but the —— Battalion still had control of the situation there.[3]

With pleasure and amusement we watched some of our field guns open up on a dozen Jerries sunbaking on the beach in the rear of their lines. One beautifully aimed shell plumped down in the midst of them, raising a cloud of sand. To our chagrin we saw them all walk away. The shell had proved a dud!

That night, I had a horrible experience. Having left C Company's HQ to return to our own headquarters atop of the hill, I missed the track. Stumbling about in pitch darkness to try and get my bearings I found myself amid a heap of dead Germans—corpses that had been lying there for three or four days. The bodies had swollen to nearly double their normal size and had literally burst from their uniforms. Wherever I walked I seemed to stand on spongy, nauseating flesh. Several times I fell over a loathsome mound, the stink of which made me vomit. When, finally, I worked my way to headquarters I felt as though I had lived through a nightmare.

In the morning we learned that the battalion guarding the airfield in the east had captured the olive-oil factory. Two British

I tanks, which nobody had seemed to know of, had led the attack. They crashed the gate and were followed in by the infantry. The stanchions supporting the top floor of the building had been smashed and the whole thing collapsed, bringing fifty-odd Jerries down with it.

News also came from the Retimo front, where the enemy had retreated to the outskirts of the town and dug themselves in between the mountains and the sea.

Mustered within our own lines were some 550 prisoners, with several of whom we had an interesting talk. A surprising fact was that so many of them spoke English. The majority were aged from eighteen to twenty-three, and admitted that they had made jumps in Holland, Norway and France during the battles of the previous year. The average age of officers was thirty, and one of them was heard to boast that not they, but we, would be the prisoners very soon.

These paratroops had been told in Athens that they would meet with very little resistance.

3

TANK FIASCO

The presence of the two tanks evidently had an influence upon the strategic position,[1] for after a conference at Battalion HQ it was decided that an attack should be launched at 6 a.m. next day (26 May) against the enemy lines at Retimo. The tanks were to lead, one along the beach and the other over the foothills. Though both were veterans of the desert, where they had been knocked out, they had been hastily patched up, quarter-inch steel being substituted for five-inch.

Our infantry moved through the village at five o'clock and took up their position at the starting point. Half an hour later one of the tanks crunched along the road, passed the village and halted. If this attack succeeded we should have been able to move down to Suda Bay. But something seemed to have gone wrong. At six o'clock, the men were seen streaming back, looking rather dejected. We were told that the assault had been cancelled because one of the tanks had broken down and the other had slipped off the edge of the road and bogged itself. However, one company was left out in front.

From eight o'clock onwards the Germans put on their customary strafing and it was evening before we were able to bring up a 75 mm gun from the eastern perimeter and put it into action on the hill facing Retimo. Stores, chiefly ammunition, were landed during the night from an invasion barge and successfully transported to our lines.

Our attack had not been cancelled, but postponed. It was timed for the following morning when, according to plan, our artillery—all five guns—laid down a barrage on the German trenches. The enemy's guns also opened fire but were not directed at any particular target.

With our machine-gunners sweeping the German trenches, the tanks advanced at 6 a.m., firing as they bumped forward, one on each flank of the battalion, which contrived to push to within fifty yards of the enemy line. The Germans threw everything they had, both at the infantry and the tanks, one of which was quickly afire at the side of the road, evidently as the result of a hit from a mortar bomb. Shortly afterwards the tank on the beach was hit, one of its tracks being blown off. Simultaneously three men were seen to leap from the first tank and our infantry began to fall back before a terrible wall of fire. Clearly, our attack had failed and our casualties had been heavy.

In an attempt to prevent the capture of the tanks a company was left behind as a screen, but both wrecks were soon targets for the dive-bombers. We learned later that one of the tank gunners, to cover the escape of his comrades, had remained at his post, where he perished in the flames. It was not until after nightfall that the infantry out in front launched a mock attack and rescued the crew from the other wreck on the beach under murderous fire. An infantry corporal distinguished himself by running straight at a battery of Jerry machine-guns and letting the crews have burst after burst from the Bren which he carried at his hip. He paid with his life, and his body remained slumped in a kneeling position supported by his gun. By then we had lost about half our men, most of them having been killed.

On the 28th we heard that C Company had made a surprise frontal attack and had passed right through the German lines, drawing fire from some houses behind. There was a rumour that both battalions would move forward during the day but it was not substantiated. The air blitz continued as ferociously as ever but, apart from this, conditions on the ground were very quiet. Apparently both sides had reached the stage when they were pinned down for lack of men. Whoever got reinforcements first would be the winners. As for us, except for the arrival of the one barge, we were out of communication with the rest of the island.

Before dawn next day, those who were left of C Company fought their way back to our lines without their brave commander. He had been killed and his body lay in the enemy lines.

There was no shutting our eyes to the dismal prospect. Food rations were very low and our men were showing signs of weariness. An order to withdraw, late in the afternoon, therefore caused no surprise. By sundown we had dragged our guns back to the eastern perimeter of the aerodrome and were soon bedded down for the night.

As soon as it was light enough to see the infantry got down to the job of digging in around the edge of the landing field, and we took our little two-pounder across it to cover the road as an anti-tank defence. As the hours passed all our positions came under heavy artillery bombardment—the heaviest pasting they had yet received. My view of the road was obscured by a bend. In fact, I could see no more than 200 yards. This did not worry me much, for I had only two rounds of ammunition left. The fellows were growing restless and there was a disturbing air of uncertainty everywhere.

At 8 a.m. a tank rumbled round the bend of the road. I hastily loaded and was squinting over the sights when I saw another tank and then two more—four tanks of medium type marked with the ominous black cross. Before I could take in the situation the tanks were blazing away with everything they had. There was nothing to do. I abandoned the gun and took cover. All around me, the infantry were firing, not at the tanks but at a stream of motorcyclists following them. Our Vickers gunners swept the approaching enemy from end to end, and might have stopped the attack had the Jerries not succeeded in bringing some small howitzers into action and been opportunely reinforced. It was the end.

Two officers from A Battalion's lines walked out waving a white towel, though there was still firing from both sides.[2]

4

SURRENDER

From mouth to mouth the order passed to drop our arms and surrender, but this was qualified within a few minutes by an intimation that we could make a dash for the hills if we wished. After a hurried discussion as to which would be the better course, some of us started out along the creek bed. Shells were exploding like crackers and we had covered only a short distance when two of our lads went down. Crawling and running we got perhaps 200 yards away when we were halted by German machine-gunners who had infiltrated to our rear. Desperately sheering off to a flank we were brought up with a round turn by tanks and infantry. The attempt to escape was useless. We

Officers of the German relief force holding a conference before the final assault on Retimo.

were surrounded, and Jerry was busily mopping-up. Either we surrendered or we would face massacre. Accepting the inevitable, we made our way to the ration dump and began to eat. It was then exactly nine o'clock.

Our meal was interrupted by the advent of half a dozen Germans who came up to us from different directions. One of them, apparently an NCO, informed us in good English that we were prisoners of the Reich. We were ordered to keep our hands above our heads and follow him. Ten minutes later we filed on to the aerodrome and were systematically relieved of everything in our pockets. Too dejected to care what was happening we found ourselves in the company of about 100 of our fellows as forlorn as we.

The enemy troops here were Austrian Alpines wearing an almost sky-blue uniform. They were a solid looking lot.

All sound of fighting had ceased, the dreadful quietness being broken only by the persistent drone of everlasting planes. Secure in their victory the Nazis had taken off their steel helmets and were wearing long-peaked 'jockey caps'. Colonel ——,[1] our senior officer, was in earnest conversation with a young German officer, evidently the enemy commander.

It was a bitter moment when we saw our German prisoners released and our wounded collected and carried away in trucks. But we were not given much time for repining. A detachment of push-bike troops was substituted for our former guards and we found ourselves shuffling along the road towards Retimo.

The fields on each side were sprinkled with dead and no-man's-land near the town itself was even more thickly spread with corpses. Nearer the lines formerly occupied by the enemy bodies had been cleared from the roadway and heaped three and four deep in the gutters. We saw a paratrooper, still attached to his parachute, hanging from the telephone wires. Half his head had been blown off.

Our two tanks were where we had seen them last, and in front of the one on the beach the gallant corporal still knelt in death. Nobody had disturbed him. How he must have haunted those Huns during the past four days!

Wherever we looked were the ghastly relics of a battle field. Over them brooded a silence so solemn that the tramp of our feet seemed a sacrilege. Even in the town there was no respite for there, sad-faced Greeks were searching the fire-blackened ruins for their lost ones. Along the footpaths the bodies of women and children lay in neat rows, their only pall being the stinking smoke which continued to belch from the smouldering olive-oil factory.

The Germans were not in the least affected by the tragedy of the scene. They strode through the streets like conquering heroes or peered laughing from the windows of houses. When our column halted in front of the schoolhouse they did not hesitate to jeer at us. Some spat upon us; others aimed kicks at us. We were helpless to do anything about it.

Eventually, however, we were allowed inside the school and were left at rest until six o'clock next morning, when we were kicked out of the corners in which we had slept. A handful of raisins was given to each man and we were warned that this was the ration for the day. We gulped down those raisins like wild beasts. They were the first food we had had for twenty-four hours.

When we had been mustered on the road the guards drove us along like a herd of cattle. All-told, there were perhaps 400 Australians and 1,000 Greeks. Hardly a man was in a fit condition to march, but march we did under a burning sun and with parched mouths. Those who could not stand the pace dropped in their tracks, but the stronger fellows glued their eyes on the road in the hope of picking up cigarette ends or something edible. We dreaded each village for as soon as we appeared we were spat at, jeered at and beaten up by the truculent Nazis in occupation.[2]

At noon we were permitted to rest for an hour by a stream. The men were so hungry that they pounced upon dried orange peel which had been in the dirt for weeks.

It was not until eight o'clock at night that we trudged exhaustedly into Georgiopolous, which was a mere burnt-out shell. Here we paused for an hour before stumbling onwards

A German photograph of the surrender at Retimo. The author is the soldier in the lower left corner.

over seemingly endless miles. At 11 p.m., when we felt that we could no longer drag one foot after another, we were halted and told that we could sleep. No food was issued and we had no blankets. Almost insensible with fatigue and hunger, we sank down where we were.

As early as half-past three in the morning we were roused and forced once again to resume our terrible march. Our stomachs were empty and our nerves on edge. Since leaving Retimo we had seen little evidence of fighting. We had been on our feet for some seven hours when, just as we approached a little village, a skinny fowl darted into the road. As one man, those in the leading row fell upon it and tearing it to pieces, ate it, feathers and all, on the spot. We were all hungry and weak and by this time several who had collapsed under the strain had been left behind by the roadside. None felt that he could go on much longer. Soon, however, the scenery grew more familiar. We found ourselves just behind Kalevis, about five miles from Suda Bay, and amid grim evidence of hard fighting. Lying where they had been shot down were the bodies of Australian, New Zealand and British troops. Suddenly, on rounding a bend we came upon a grisly group of five Aussies prone upon the ground in natural positions. Not one of them showed any sign of having been hit. Yet, judging by the sickening stench which came from their bodies, they had been dead for at least a week. Apparently the Germans had collected and buried the corpses of their own comrades for we did not see any.

It was two o'clock in the afternoon when we staggered, practically at our last gasp, into Suda Bay, where the damage left us speechless. The harbour was studded with the wrecks of sunken craft, some of which were still smoking. Though the wharf and installations were intact, nothing at all remained of the village. It was a mound of rubble. Our time to take in the scene was short, for we were herded into a compound and divided into working parties. Several raucous-voiced Germans took control of each party and soon we were carrying 300-pound bags of English rice from the store to the wharf. How we did so, I will never know; but we did.

A wounded German paratrooper rejoins his own troops after the surrender at Retimo.

At 7 p.m. we were marched back to the pen and lined up for a ration of food. Jerry handed out a British 12-ounce tin of bully beef for every eight men, and some biscuits. As there were not sufficient of the latter to go round, the lucky beggars at the front end of the line were the only ones to receive them. Nevertheless, one of our cooks achieved a miracle by making half a pound of tea serve the needs of over 1,000 men. Afterwards the tea leaves were dried and smoked by such as had the good fortune to get within reach of them.

Dawn saw us again in working parties and again humping rice. In our famished state we used our wits. Whenever we could do so unobserved we slit the bags, filled our pockets with rice and swallowed it raw, little by little.[3]

One special party had been selected to bury German dead. The members were humanely issued with respirators.

Early in the afternoon there were signs of excitement among the Germans. We quickly discovered the reason. Three freighters of about 5,000 tons had entered the harbour and were making ready to berth at the wharf. Their decks were cluttered with mobile kitchens and field workshops, but in the holds, no doubt, were much-needed stores. If so, we were not destined to share them, for by evening we were on the move towards Canea, the second largest town on the island. It was hard going for us. The road had been severely bombed and was full of holes. Most of the dead on either side seemed to have been buried, but we passed one German corpse without a stitch of clothing. The numerous wounds on the body suggested that he must have been struck by several bursts of machine-gun fire.

A large British hospital at the approaches to Canea had plainly been subjected to very heavy bombing. As for the town, it was, like Retimo, a place of death and desolation. We could smell the ungathered dead among the ashes and debris, and the streets, except for some groups of loitering Germans, were deserted.

We reached the General Military Hospital at 10 p.m. It was situated five miles beyond Canea and the Germans had thrown barbed wire around the perimeter and converted it into a prison camp.

Here we were given a mug of tea and a biscuit each and took our places among a mixed bag of Australian, New Zealand, English, Scottish, Greek and Palestinian troops as well as sailors, marines and airmen.

5

BATTLE AFTERMATH

An early morning swim in the sea, which touched the camp on one side, put new life into us.[1] This was just as well because we were paraded immediately afterwards and ordered to march to Maleme.

The road wound parallel to the beach and as the miles slowly went by it became more and more evident that we were trekking through a huge cemetery. Every few hundred yards we passed graves, in some of which as many as twenty bodies had been interred. The Germans had honoured their fallen comrades by covering their resting places with white chipped marble and bordering them with cement. There was a black cross for each man inscribed with his name, number, regiment and the date on which he had been killed. And at the foot of each cross was a helmet.

No such tribute had been paid to their enemies. The bodies of our poor chaps had been dumped into the ditches by the roadside and some earth—but not enough—had been heaped over them. Here and there we would see a ghastly fist or a foot sticking out. And instead of ornate crosses, rifles had been up-ended by plunging the bayonets into the ground. So lay our cobbers.

Rounding a headland, we at last caught a glimpse of the Maleme aerodrome and the litter that bespoke the fierce conflict that had raged there. The airfield itself was rectangular—some 600 by 300 yards of yellow clay reaching to the water's edge. From end to end the whole area was a jumble of wrecked aircraft. It resembled a colossal junk-heap. Though we were still two miles away the spectacle was staggering.

Entering a small village,[2] we came upon a British light tank upside-down in the middle of the street. How it had got into that position was a complete mystery for we could find no trace of damage upon it. And on the beach, not far distant, was another puzzling sight. Less than fifty yards apart, and facing one another, were a British Hurricane and a German Messerschmitt 109. Beside each plane was a grave.

When we were within two or three hundred yards of the aerodrome the real lesson of destruction was brought home to us. We gazed upon a terrific tangle of metal and aerial flotsam. All that remained of several hundreds of planes was spread

Australian and New Zealand prisoners of war on the march to Maleme.

before our eyes. Most of them, apparently, had been three-engined Junkers transports. The remainder were a mixed lot of Dorniers, Heinkels, Messerschmitts and Stukas. They formed a mass of tortured confusion and it was not difficult to judge why. Our guns had pumped hell into them.[3]

Arriving in the village of Maleme, on the edge of the airfield, we veered off at right-angles to a spot behind the battered church, where we found ourselves in a new prison camp. During the past four days we had marched over sixty miles and done a lot of work, besides. Every man of us was in the last stage of exhaustion. We could not have walked another step; we could have worked no more.

Yet, there was to be little respite. It seemed that we had barely

closed our eyes when the guards turned us out at sunrise and detailed us to working parties, each numbering about fifty. Escorted by five soldiers, my party was sent to the aerodrome— to the western end where dozens of ruined gliders presented their more or less damaged frames for our inspection. First, we were set to work clearing the runway of debris and filling-in the clotted shell-holes. The guards drove us relentlessly and objected with hoarse roars and cruel kicks to even a minute's rest.

But they could not stop us from talking. We were told by other prisoners that the New Zealand troops, assisted by Marines and Australians, had strenuously and at great sacrifice defended the field to the last.[4]

As our labours took us from place to place we came across several British Bofors AA guns on the perimeter, and at the western boundary of the field were two battered Blenheim bombers. Incidentally, some of the Bofors were still intact.

A few biscuits were issued to us at noon and we were allowed to sit about for an hour, but promptly at one o'clock the guards were driving us again and we were kept hard at the job, although the heat was like a furnace, until dusk.

Then, carefully counted, we were marshalled back to the camp. There were no tents. There were no blankets. We sprawled where we could, trying our best to fend off the frightful smell that drifted from the adjoining camp in which several thousands of unfortunate Greeks were confined.

Most of us had given up the idea of food when, at 8 p.m., rations were issued. These consisted of one twelve-ounce tin of bully beef to eight men and half a biscuit a man. In a mood of desperation, hardly caring what our captors might think, we grouped in parties of twelve. Pooling what we had been served and adding a few lentils which some of the smarter ones had managed to scrounge, we made a watery stew. The luckier lads who had been successful during the day in locating cigarette ends enjoyed the luxury of a 'smoke'.

The next day proved to be a repetition of the one before, except that we had now carved enough space out of the airfield to enable transport planes to land and take off. My own party was allotted the duty of unloading and reloading these machines. We noticed that the incoming cargoes[5] consisted chiefly of food and that the outgoing freight was mainly wounded Germans.

Still—and I must admit this—we were surprised at eleven o'clock in the morning to see about fifty of our badly wounded comrades loaded aboard and to hear from them that they had been very well treated.

Jerry ran these transport aircraft like a taxi service. Ten Planes would land, unload, reload and take off in an hour, and needless to say, we found the job more interesting than pick-and-shovel graft.[5]

Returning, at length, to our nightly bully beef and biscuits, we began to sum up our amenities. That did not take long. For example, there was only one well to provide drinking water, and the Greeks shared it with us—more than 3,500 men crowding around for a drink of filthy water. For bathing and washing there was a sewerage drain with about eighteen inches of water in it.[6] However, a few of us had acquired a blanket each or an old coat and were thankful for the protection it gave us from the chill.

That night, all our officers but one—a doctor—were lined-up and warned that they must be ready to march out at five in the morning. We noticed that the Germans had decided upon sterner measures of supervision. They mounted double guards, and the sentries were wearing steel helmets.

We saw the last of the officers at daybreak. They left under a strong escort, and from what we overheard they were to be flown to Germany.

As for us, in addition to unloading the aerial transports, a large gang was set to building a jetty. Dysentery, however, was beginning to play havoc among us and some of its victims were already too weak to walk more than a few yards. In vain the doctor asked for drugs to treat the disease. The prison commandant told him they were unprocurable. Most of us were like living skeletons and as our strength ebbed, so did our spirits. The latrines were occupied twenty-four hours a day.

Food had become so short that even the Jerries were feeling

the pinch. On 7 June a party of twenty of us, with ten guards, was instructed to ransack the surrounding villages and requisition everything that could be eaten. But without exception, the hamlets were either deserted or in ashes. Such inhabitants as had not been killed had long since fled to the hills. All we could find was an occasional pig and a few scrawny fowls, the sole survivors of a ravaged countryside.

Next day I was withdrawn from my usual plane-loading and sent to join the jetty gang, who sweated under the all-seeing eye of a German civil engineer—a bulky giant well over six feet tall garbed in plus-fours. Our task was to carry big rocks from a heap and drop them in the water fifty yards from the shore. 'Hermann', as we dubbed the boss, had his own method of stimulating our enthusiasm. Any man who lagged or faltered was belaboured across the shoulders with a piece of timber!

While we were thus occupied another party was kept busy unloading steel railway tracks from a schooner which had come round from Suda Bay.

This was not an easy or agreeable job, but it was certainly a happier one than fell to those of our mates who were obliged to act as batmen to the German officers. One particular officer insisted upon four men waiting upon him!

Yet I decided to swallow my pride rather than endure the crushing toil of carrying stones for the jetty. I attached myself to the corps of batmen next day, and found the work quite luxurious. All I had to do was to clean the 'master's' tent, serve his meals, and follow wherever he led. There were no guards to bother me and I was able to acquire a few cigarettes. To our surprise most of the officers spoke pretty good English and conversed freely with us.

The fellow to whom I was attached did his best to convince us that the German soldier was a superman. When we refused to agree with him he compromised and reluctantly admitted that the Anzacs were the toughest fighters he had come up against. But he stood firm in the conviction that Germany would win the war and was explicit as to what would happen to Australia when peace was signed. He promised that our national living conditions would be improved on the Nazi model and that, except for this, the only difference in our economy would be that our raw materials would be shipped to the Reich instead of to Britain.

On the following night the padre who had been left with us organised a cheer-up concert. Quite a few of the guards were in the audience and seemed to enjoy the programme, the more modern of our songs seeming to interest them especially. This, it seemed, was because topical popular songs had been banned from the Fatherland since 1936. The Jerries did what they could, however, by rendering their regimental 'Paratroopers' Song' and the inevitable 'Horst Wessel'.[7]

There was no doubt about their smartness on parade. We would see them march along the road bellowing a rousing chorus. They would suddenly become silent on approaching the parade ground and, at a strident order from their commanding officer, change perfectly into the goose step. We had to admit that they made an impressive picture.

My cushy job soon came to an end and I was once again hard at it loading and unloading transport planes. It was monotonous work and the time dragged endlessly. Incidentally, these huge machines were apparently difficult to ground. Scarcely a day had passed without at least one crashing. On the outward journey they were now carrying Nazi troops to Athens en route to Berlin on furlough.

Dysentery was spreading amongst us, but the doctor had neither leisure nor medicine to spend on us. He was concentrating upon more serious cases. There had been so much sickness that by 12 June only about half our original number remained in camp.

The food had not improved. Indeed, some of the concoctions we had to swallow tasted and looked bad enough to kill us. Many meals comprised a morsel of beef in water with a spinkling of olive leaves to make the mixture look like stew! After one such repast I spent an entire day at the latrine trench.

When I had the strength to crawl about again I was made assistant to a German armourer who figured among various technicians engaged in salvaging anything worthwhile from the accumulated plane wreckage. The pair of us recovered a number of machine-guns and, for me, the job was not without interest. My temporary boss proved rather easy-going despite the fact that he was never without his Luger. On the second day, after some dismantling work on a Messerschmitt 110, he gave me three cigarettes and a biscuit.

It was obvious that we Australians had been treated, in general, with more respect than some of the other prisoners. The hardest and most irksome duties were allotted to the British and Greeks and their guards did not hesitate to beat them up. On one occasion three Greeks and a Tommy were made to stand on one leg holding a heavy stone over their heads until they collapsed. So far as we could see this was purely for the entertainment of the guards.[8]

6

AN IDEA IS BORN

By 24 June I had made up my mind that rather than go mad or die of slow starvation I would try to make a break. After all, a burst of machine-gun bullets would be better than the torture of fading out gradually in this filthy pen.

There were, of course, a lot of 'ifs'. The camp, with its barbed-wire fences and alert guards, was a problem in itself. Covering each corner were concealed machine-guns, and each side was patrolled by two sentries.

Even assuming that one could escape, what then? The closest British posts were 300 miles away, separated from Crete by 280 miles of open water. Would it be possible to steal a boat? Was the local population pro-British or pro-Nazi?[1] These were some of the questions to be faced.

However, with the idea of freedom at the back of my mind, I started to keep a close watch on the movements of the guards, using the latrines as my chief observation post. I also succeeded in stealing a pair of wire-cutters from a tool kit and smuggled them, with a few handfuls of dirty biscuits, to a hiding place.

Two other lads talked of attempting to escape, but I kept my own intentions to myself, and laughed openly at theirs. Everybody seemed to think it would be a practical impossibility to get away. To me it was damnable to see these cobbers of mine, the finest men to leave Australia, lying or staggering about in this unholy compound. They were visibly rotting before my eyes—just so many animated skeletons, but still with enough spirit in them to laugh and joke.

I had been doing some deep thinking and deemed it advisable, after all, to approach the two who had mentioned their desire to escape.[2] A quiet talk convinced us that it would be best to join forces. One of the lads had found a prismatic compass which might come in useful and all three of us scrounged for anything edible to augment our slender supplies. And, of course, there was further intensive study of the guards.

The great decision was made on 28 June. We committed ourselves to make the dash that evening.

The time was fixed for six o'clock, for, though darkness did not come down until three hours later, we had noticed that the guards relaxed towards the end of the day.

At a muster parade in the morning every man in camp was handed a form and ordered to write down his name, number, rank, next-of-kin and civilian occupation. Without exception we decided to be 'farmers'.

We three in the escape plot were strung to a condition of nervous tension. It seemed to us that the guards were more numerous and vigilant than before. I, for one, was relieved when a fourth man asked if he might join in the attempt.[3] So, there we were—Flap, Fred, Blue and myself—keying ourselves up for the jump. We realised we would need a lot of luck.

Strangely, we were given ample time for thought. Too much, perhaps. There were no working parties required and we were free to laze about in the sun. The packing of our small bundles was quickly over and, as the critical moment drew near, we took all who remained of our own particular crowd into our confidence. This was the first they had heard of the scheme. Immediately, of course we were pressed to let the whole bunch join in, and it was with difficulty that we could convince them that four was the maximum number that could hope to get out. I felt very guilty. There was not one of these boys who did not present a picture of misery and suffering. There was not one who had not as much right to freedom as we.

The section of the fence we were to go through was nearest the hills, at a point where the sewer drain took a bend. When the moment came I rolled four feet into the bottom of the irrigation drain and wriggled round the bend which partly screened us from the guard and waited, breathless, for my three companions. We lay there for several minutes and then slowly I climbed the wall of the drain and snipped the lowest strand of barbed wire. I glanced nervously in both directions but the guards had their backs to us and I hissed to the others to crawl through the fence.

I followed and as I elbowed my way under the wire I saw one of the guards half turn. I froze momentarily—but he had not seen me—and reached the open grass beyond. I covered the ten yards which separated me from the vineyard in record time and dived for cover.

But we had tricked ourselves. We realised at once that if we moved we would be under observation both from the camp and the guardhouse beyond. As the ground sloped upwards, there would be no possibility of evading discovery. The alternative was to lie precisely where we were until dark, a full three hours hence.

After half an hour's interminable suspense, the clang of a bell rang out. This would be the alarm. Hugging the earth, we waited breathlessly for what might come, almost feeling in advance the thump of bullets. Then came the noise of voices and pounding boots. The searchers came within five yards of us, and passed on.

Another hour, like a lifetime, passed. Suddenly, the silence was split by the angry chatter of a machine-gun. Had we been discovered? Would it be better to stand up and surrender? These questions rushed to our minds and drew the sweat from our skins. But we did not stir. We tried not to blink even an eyelid.

And so the minutes came and went, until, at length, sick with the strain, we saw with relief that it was growing steadily darker. A slight breeze rustled through the bushes and cooled our damp bodies.

Slowly and softly, yard by yard, we wormed our way up the hillside, pausing often to listen. By the time we reached the summit it was quite dark, though not too opaque to prevent us seeing a bitumen road and some olive groves on the other side of it.

A heavy truck, with two glaring headlights, sent us to earth, but it had no sooner rumbled by than we spurted towards the olive bushes, with but one thought—to get as far away from camp and pursuit as we could. We crept and ran until we panted for breath, each snapping twig or falling stone bringing us to a frightened halt. On the outskirts of a village our presence roused every dog in the place to excited barking. Without a second's hesitation, we turned in our tracks and ran for an hour without stopping.

It must have been about three in the morning when we found ourselves in rough hill country. We were so deadly tired that we decided to risk an hour or two of sleep. Our endurance was virtually at an end.

Our sleep was like death itself. Complete oblivion. It was not until five-thirty that I awoke, just as daylight was reddening the horizon. Rousing my companions I took stock of the surroundings. We overlooked a semi-circular valley at the bottom of which a beautiful stream gurgled an invitation to us to wash. As there was nobody to be seen we decided to go down and then push south until we struck the coast. Should we meet any Greeks we would do our best to avoid them.

After several hours of steady walking we were sent to cover by a German reconnaissance plane, flying at a height of no more than 200 feet. But it went on. We had not been observed.

All was well until, on taking a turn, we encountered a black-bearded Greek. We found ourselves face to face with him and in the panic of the moment picked up stones to beat out his brains if he showed signs of making trouble. For a full minute he stared at us, and we stared back at him. Then he spoke.

'Germania?' he asked.

'English,' we replied.

Immediately a grin swept his face and he asked why we were tramping about the country.

We explained that we had escaped from the prison camp at Maleme and were trying to get to the coast.

Casually, he informed us that the track we were following would lead us into a German garrison village.[4] Would we care for some bread, cheese and wine?

AN IDEA IS BORN

Would we care! We ate what he gave us ravenously, and his wine was like nectar.

This good Samaritan then offered to conduct us to a friendly village where, on our approach, the inhabitants looked at us somewhat doubtfully until our guide shouted 'Alla Englaiseco'. Before we could lift a hand we were surrounded by all sorts who essayed to shake our hands and kiss us, all at the same time. Bread, cheese, olives and wine were pressed upon us, and we fed and drank like kings. True, the wine was as sour as vinegar, but the more we had of it the more we felt its strength. Nor would these kind people let us go until they had loaded us with bread.

7

AMONG FRIENDS

In the next two villages through which we passed, we were given the same hospitable treatment. When we came to a third, equally well disposed, we knew it was time to rest for the night. The mellow effect of 'krassy' had banished our fears. Not only that, but it had made us so sleepy that the last we remembered was being tucked into bed.

The guide told us next morning that he had resolved to take us to his own village. But first we had to say goodbye to our hosts, and a prolonged and vociferous parting it was. Then, in good heart, we set off in single file along a winding track which twisted up hill and down dale against a grandiose background of purple, snow-capped ranges. In consideration of our physical weakness, the Greek kept the pace slow.

There was an alarming moment early in the afternoon, when a party of Germans was spied ahead of us at the bottom of a valley. Our courageous friend said we were to stay in hiding until he assured us that it was safe to go on. He left us for ten minutes and went down boldly to brave the lions in their den. We could see the Germans questioning him. But he was evidently able to find out more than they did, for when he returned he whispered that they were a patrol sent out to search the villages.

We reached our destination by a circuitous route just after nightfall, and were welcomed by the guide's family, who were apparently still excited by the fact that the house had been 'gone over' by the enemy twice during the day. But that did not affect the warmth of their greeting nor the excellence of the food they provided for us. During the meal, the family was joined by three picturesque fellows with curled moustaches. They were wearing ragged Greek uniforms, and according to our guides were brothers. Having fought in Albania, they had escaped to Crete.

There was then a conference, the upshot of which was that we were advised to lie low for a week or two. The family knew of just the place for us. And so, loaded with rations and blankets we left this friendly roof eventually to find ourselves, after a hard trek, in a copse cosily situated in a pocket just below the tip of a high mountain. Here we were destined to stay for the next ten days.

Far below nestled the small white cottages of a village, above which a road writhed like a black serpent. In perfect weather our eyes met beauty in every direction, the very air being scented with the perfume of wild herbs and the rich crops of distant farms. Here and there, amid the luscious green of trees and flowering bushes, sparkling streams weaved gaily down the valleys.[1] Against all was the background of an endless chain of mountains. It was impossible to associate war with this panorama of peace and loveliness; impossible to associate human slaughter and strife with the life of the goatherd and his family who lived in a hut halfway down our mountainside. The music of the goat bells mingled soothingly with the songs of these happy, harmless people, attuning our thoughts to all that was best and good.

Every day was a day of joy and relaxation; every day food and wine would be brought to us. However, we had a feeling that this brief happiness could not last. On 8 July we debated whether we should move on or stay where we were a little longer. Personally, I favoured making our way towards the sea, whatever the risk might be, but I was overruled. An excited Greek ran to us next with the warning that we must get out. Word had been passed to the mayor of the district—a pro-German—that four British soldiers were hiding in the hills. We were compelled to escape while there was time.

In no two minds about accepting this advice, we started at dusk, still under the guidance of faithful friends who saw that

we were given a substantial meal in a village a few miles off
before bidding us 'adios'.[2]

We spent the rest of the night and all the following day in
a large garden orchard below the village, eating fruit when we
felt like it, and sleeping. At nightfall an elderly Greek appeared
and said he would put us in a place where no German would
ever locate us. Moreover, he was as good as his word for, after
a pleasant interval in a village where we were regaled with supper
and wine, we were taken to a small gully running down the side
of a steep hill. The spot seemed remote and there was ample
cover. But although everything appeared to be all right and we
had more than sufficient food, I was not easy in my mind. I
told my comrades that I would leave for the coast even if I had
to go by myself. It was for them to make their choice. They did.

After sunset on the 11th I gathered some bread and cheese,
shook hands with the lads and commenced my lonely journey.
It was understood between us that I should wait for a week at
a predetermined spot so that the others might join me should
they change their minds.[3]

On leaving the gully I headed south, across country, my
immediate goal being some fifteen miles distant. I was lucky
enough to pick up a lad of fifteen who knew the countryside
well. He was agreeable to accompany me. But what a pilgrimage
that was! For hours on end we climbed and slid over the roughest
terrain imaginable until I began to regret that I had not delayed
my departure until daylight. Halfway to my destination we were
forced to rest and sank down to sleep under some thick bushes.
Almost frozen, I awoke at dawn to find my boy guide already
eager to push on. He indicated that there was no time to waste,
and so off we were again. Having negotiated a small settlement
and a stream we ascended a range and took a careful look
around.[4] Virtually at the same instant we spotted a convoy
winding along a road far below us. It consisted of forty-five
motor cycle and sidecar outfits and a dozen heavy trucks.

Slipping down the other side of the incline I caught a distant
view of the sea—a heartening sight, if ever there was one.

After trudging for three full hours we halted at a village and were offered hospitality.[5] Some of the inhabitants told me that there were already five other Australians and a New Zealander there. If I would like to talk to them a guide would conduct me to their hiding place. Naturally, I was only too happy to accept the offer.

These half-dozen fugitives proved a ferocious-looking lot. They were unshaven, ragged, dirty and, judging by their manner, rather desperate. Several, it appeared, had escaped from a prison camp at Canea, and the others had never been captured. They said they had searched the coast for twenty miles but had been unable to find a boat of any description. At least, none that would float. However, they knew of one spot where several craft were under guard.

Guarded or not, I thought it would be a good idea to investigate the position. There was always the chance that circumstances, or luck, might not favour the Germans. As soon as I put this point of view forward one of the chaps agreed with me. He said he would take the risk with me.

Eventually we left the others to themselves and marched off down a track which, within an hour or so, brought us to a large village entirely free of the enemy.[6] We entered the first cafe we came across and were quickly in conversation with several English-speaking Greeks. To our great surprise we learned that two New Zealanders—one of them a Maori named Bill—were sheltering there. Although cigarettes were valued at about five shillings each and were almost unprocurable even at that price we were both handed half a one and treated to several glasses of wine. 'Bill' and his friend then materialised and we had quite a long talk with them before being claimed by a young Greek who insisted that we should sleep at his father's house. There, with sighs of contentment, we spent a peaceful night.

Waking with the dawn we saw that we were in a tiny village, white and pretty in the rays of the rising sun. The air was pervaded with the smell of olive oil cooking—a smell which effectively roused us from our lethargy. We just had time to enjoy a brisk and icy wash when we were required to go through the lengthy ceremonial of being introduced to the twenty or so members of the family, who all appeared to be cheerful, decent folk.

Because Bob, my companion in escapism, went down with colic my sojourn extended to seven days. Bob was so ill at one stage that our Greek friend felt obliged to produce a doctor who, though his exterior might not have pleased the BMA, was worthy of his cure. While the patient was recovering I helped the villagers to pick the almond crops and hoe potatoes. Actually, Bob was up and about again in five days. Our young Greek, who spent most of his hours spying for Germans, then took us both for a drink—a potent spirit brewed from walnuts and tasting like gin.[7] In two more days Bob was back to normal. However, when I proposed that we should get moving again, he declined to budge. He said that as these people had been so kind he would stay with them.

It was, of course, well over seven days since I had left my three original companions, and as there had been no sign of them, no word or message, I felt free to wander on my own. But where? Somewhat inexplicably I was seized with the notion of making my way back to Retimo. It was at least an objective.

I made good progress. I followed a dry river course until I located a path spiralling thousands of feet up a mountain. When the sun was going down I came upon a village—the same sort of village as many previous ones, and I am proud to pay my humble tribute to their spirit—which gave me a hearty welcome. These Greek people were incredible. They were ready to accept the risk of any terrorism and punishment on our behalf.

A great, bearded Cretan, garbed in the traditional dress, pleaded with me to stay with him at least for a few days. His home was built on the edge of a cliff whence you could look over a wide and splendid landscape. Even the village itself loomed as a jewel. In their setting, the whitewashed little houses, overlooking the blue Mediterranean, with a jagged blue background of mountains, gleamed like a picture.

Upon entering the cottage I was introduced to my host's wife and two daughters. They expressed in their demeanour all that I loved of Greece. All together, and in the most amiable spirits, we dined on goat's milk, herb broth, and pancakes cooked in olive oil, washed down with copious draughts of wine.

This Cretan was a simple man, accustomed to a simple life. He did not understand the war and, on principle, did not like Germans. Luckily, I had a few photos of persons dear to me in my pockets. He was particularly interested in one of my sweetheart. As none of the family spoke English, however, the situation was somewhat strained. But, by a miracle, I was able to impress upon them that such-and-such was my affianced girl.

'Poly kalore,' they all chortled. That meant 'very good'.

With the Cretan and two of his dogs for company I slept that night on the roof, wrapped in one of the gaudiest rugs the household could produce. In the morning I spent some interesting hours strolling from house to house, watching the various families at their work. It seemed that every child, every goat and every dog was determined to escort me.

Though the Greek hours of eating—the first meal of the day being at noon, and the second and last at about ten o'clock at night—were not to my taste, I returned 'home' for lunch, to find that a special dish had been prepared for me. This proved to be flowers of marrow stuffed with rice and barley and baked in olive oil.

Much to the disappointment of my kindly host and his family, I decided to resume my journey and set off down the valley which I knew led to the sea. He accompanied me part of the way and as we parted he gave me the traditional bread and cheese wrapped in clean white linen.

8

TO SEIZE A BOAT

It was late in the day when I arrived at the small fishing village where I had agreed to meet Flap, Fred and Blue.[1] With my usual caution I did not enter the village immediately but circled around the outskirts, watching carefully for any sign of danger.

The seaward side of the village had a fringe of wind-blown tamarisk trees under which I was excited to see two small wooden fishing boats. I made a mental note of this find, remembering my main purpose of escaping was to leave Crete and reach Egypt. The thought did pass through my mind that these were indeed small boats to undertake an open sea voyage of 280 miles.

About an hour before sunset I walked casually into the village square, which was dominated by a white church and a large drinking trough and fountain. A priest in long flowing black gown and a flat-topped brimless hat stepped out of the church entrance but he passed me without a glance. Otherwise the square appeared to be deserted. I was about to leave when I observed two Cretans seated under the bamboo awning of a coffee shop. I joined them at their table and as I sat down the taller of the two men leant forward and said, 'You look like an Aussie to me'.

Dick, for that was the man's name,[2] had fought with an Australian anti-aircraft battery at Maleme, escaped to the mountains when the battle ended and for the past two or three months had been living in the nearby villages. The meeting sparked off an unusual adventure with an almost tragic ending.

We remained in the village for three days, hoping that my

comrades from the prisoner-of-war camp would put in an appearance. During this time Dick told me he had sighted a German patrol boat along the coast at the fishing port of Paleochora. This was the base for a combined enemy army and navy force which was responsible for patrolling the coast in this area. During daylight hours the boat cruised offshore, intercepting all fishing and other craft in these waters. It returned to port at sunset and anchored off the jetty. Perhaps of more interest, Dick said, most of the crew went ashore in the evening to carouse in the few bars and coffee houses, leaving two sentries aboard to guard the boat. Dick had watched the boat for three days and the routine did not change.

Egypt and freedom seemed very close as we set off on the twelve-mile walk over the mountains to Paleochora. However, soon after starting out I realised my companion could not keep up with the pace I set. When I commented on this he said he had touches of fever in the high country. I dismissed it from my mind and concentrated on the project ahead.

Two days later we were comfortably layed up in a cave which overlooked the town and the jetty. As Dick had predicted, the patrol boat anchored some 200 yards away from the cave and close to the jetty. As the light faded the crew tumbled into a dinghy and rowed ashore. Two sentries lounged amidships and the glow from their cigarettes defined them in the gloom.

We waited with mounting excitement until about eight-thirty and then, quickly stripping to our trousers, slipped into the water which was surprisingly cold. Swimming breaststroke, we closed in on the boat until only twenty yards separated us from the sentries. Here we stopped to observe and for the first time I had misgivings about the practicability of the operation. Our only arms were Dick's long curved Cretan knife and my small club.

The loom of the boat from water level seemed to magnify it to battleship size. I glanced at Dick. It was too dark to see the expression on his face, but somehow I knew he was thinking the same as I was—were the odds too great? However, the Germans solved the problem for us. A match flared in the entrance to a hatch below the boat's bridge. The odds were now three to one and we retired silently.

We reached the shore without mishap, crawled back to the cave and hurriedly dressed. Dick was shivering and muttered that he felt sick. As we moved to leave the cave a small searchlight on the boat swept the waters of the bay. The guards were more alert than we expected.

On leaving the cave we walked inland through a maze of thorny scrub and uneven rocks. An hour later we reached a hollow on the seaward side of the coastal range. We slumped down on the ground and fell asleep. I dozed, frozen to the bone, but after an hour I stood up and shook Dick. He groaned. His face was lathered with sweat and he was breathing in short gasps. I shook him savagely to wake him but he did not move.

Dawn was close at hand and were in an exposed position not more than three miles from the German garrison. With some difficulty I dragged Dick upright and passed one of his arms around my shoulders. My little knowledge of medical matters told me it was vital to get him to help.

The thirty hours which followed were a walking nightmare. Half carrying, half dragging, falling and slipping, I climbed the first mountain range. From the crest I scanned the valley below but there was no sign of a village or habitation of any kind. I knew I would have to descend the slope at my feet and ascend the next mountain ridge.

Although Dick was greatly underweight, probably not more than eight stone, he was a deadweight. As I dragged him down through bushes and over rocks I thought of Coleridge's Ancient Mariner with a dead albatross around his neck. It was night again when I reached a small gully about a quarter of the distance up the second mountain. I dropped Dick and fell asleep.

When I awoke in the early hours of the next morning I ate the last rusks of bread we had carried with us. I found a tiny spring and drank. I bathed Dick's face and he stirred and groaned. Setting off again I found a faint goat track and followed it with closed eyes, counting 100 paces before I stopped and rested. It must have taken seven or eight hours to reach the crest of the second range. I placed Dick on a large flat rock and looked down into the valley. In the distance I saw a cluster of white-painted houses, but they seemed so far away. I slumped to the ground and fell fast asleep in the sun.

My subconscious alarm system, which all fugitives develop, woke me with a start. Standing above me was a tall bearded Cretan. My eyes swung sharply behind him to where a ten- or twelve-year-old boy was standing holding a donkey's bridle. Draped across the saddle on the donkey's back was the inert figure of Dick. The Cretan spoke to me in English with a broad American accent.[3] He told me Dick was very sick and he was taking us to his village down in the valley. His son had discovered us some hours before, while driving their sheep to a fresh pasturage. The boy's name was Nicko.

An hour later we reached the village, which consisted of four small houses and some outhouses.[4] Dick was carried into a house and laid on the table. Two women, our host's wife and her mother, stripped Dick and commenced a diagnosis. They turned him on to his stomach and probed his back, chattering in Greek. The older woman opened his mouth and trickled a little liquid, probably rakki, down his throat. They then washed his back with the same liquid. Meanwhile the grandmother boiled half a dozen small drinking glasses in a pot.

My first experience with Cretan medical treatment came as a shock. The younger woman picked up an open razor and with practiced ease made a series of shallow incisions across Dick's back. As the blood oozed from the wounds she took one of the drinking glasses from the pot and placed it over one of the wounds. Almost immediately the suction created by the hot, wet glass drew blood and fluid. Soon all six glasses were working on Dick's back.

How long this macabre operation continued I do not know. Glasses were removed with a loud plopping sound and replaced with clean ones. From time to time the woman felt the patient's pulse and placed her ear close to the upper chest to listen to the breathing.[5]

It is possible I dozed off because I was awakened by the tall Cretan's voice. He said my companion was all right though very sick, but he would recover. Dick was still unconscious and the women had just completed painting his scored back with a white paste which smelt pungently of herbs.

Half an hour later I was sitting with my host eating a meal of beans cooked in olive oil and rusk bread when Nicko raced in the house. He shouted to his father 'Germanico!' followed by a babble of rapid Greek. There were Germans in close proximity. My host told me I must go. Nicko would guide me to a cave where I would be safe. Dick must stay in the house but he would be safe.

The cave was in a fold high on the mountain range east of the village. Nicko brought me a blanket and bread, cheese and goat's milk. I was comfortable, but after three days time began to drag. It was time I moved on and on the third night I departed.

Two days later, some twenty miles east, I saw ahead of me a village perched high on a 2000-foot conical peak.[6] A winding track led up to the village which I found consisted of about forty houses. Here, in the square, I met a Cretan of about thirty who carried in bandit fashion a huge .45 calibre revolver, a German automatic pistol and an ugly curved Cretan dagger—all stuck into the cumberbund around his waist. He made no secret of the fact that he had been living for the past ten years with a price on his head.

I spent a happy day with him rounding up a flock of milking goats and two unruly bullocks. Later I was to learn these had been stolen from villages far to the east. Despite the ugly knife scars which furrowed his face and hands I took a liking to this man.

9

MY STRANGE CAPTORS

There was a surprise for me when I went back to the village, for my ancient host sought me out and handed me a note in English, reading: 'Come with the bearer, now'.

At first I was suspicious, but as both the Cretan and my bandit pal vouched for the man who had brought the message, I agreed to go with him, but not before devouring a strange repast of pancakes filled with boiled grass.[1]

The messenger took me for a long tramp to a certain village where a group of men, including an Englishman and an Australian, awaited me.[2] When I introduced myself, I was subjected to an interrogation which lasted an hour.

The Englishman, having heard my story, asked if I had proof of my identity. Unfortunately, I could offer none, whereupon he charged me with being a German spy posing as an escaped Australian![3] I felt like killing him where he stood. Indeed, I only restrained myself from violence by reminding myself of the effect the scene might have upon the simple Greeks. Apparently as a prisoner, I was led into a house and given a meal. Greek members of the band who were not quite satisfied with my bona fides argued volubly about me for hours. I had little doubt that if they came to the wrong conclusion they would cut me to pieces without a qualm. However, I was still alive at 11 p.m. when they left, locking the door upon me as they went.

Resigning myself to the situation, which, to me, was fantastic, I stretched out on an old couch. In almost less time than it takes to tell, I was being devoured by millions of fleas. Jumping up, my attention was attracted by the sound of a movement outside. I looked round for a weapon and seized a chair. I would at least make a fight for it with anybody proved nasty. But there was no further noise. I waited an hour. The silence remained unbroken. It would be safe then, I thought, to make a move. Feeling my way along the wall I touched a door, which, to my amazement, swung open. I crept out and found an open-air kitchen surrounded by a high wall. At one end was a creolie— a threshing pit—into which, highly appreciative of the good warm straw, I insinuated my weary frame. My troubles were quickly banished by sleep.

I was awakened by the heat of the morning sun to see two black-bearded Greekos surveying me not altogether with relish. They made it quite clear that they intended to keep me under surveillance, but I was nevertheless given to understand that I could walk about the village under their escort. On the whole, they behaved remarkably well. So long as they could hover in the background they were apparently well satisfied.

That night, I exchanged my old creolie for another, and in doing so, acted on second thoughts, for the Greekos had, so to speak, tucked me snugly into the original. Some hours before dawn, I came to my senses and realised I was half frozen. There was not a soul to be seen, not a sound. This, I told myself, was the chance I had been waiting for.

I crept along the high wall of the yard to a spot where I had noticed a small window about seven feet from the ground. I gripped the ledge, raised myself to the level of the aperture and wriggled through. Hanging head-down I could not see what lay below. I released my grip and plunged down a steep slope of what I later found to be scree—loose, sharp stones. How far I fell I will never know. For some minutes I lay stunned, my fall had been arrested by a stunted olive tree. Some hundreds of feet above me, silhouetted against the sky, was the village. Below, the ground fell away steeply as far as I could see.

Wriggling to a sitting position I felt my limbs, but except for abrasions and bruises I did not appear to be seriously injured.

Uncertain as to whether my fall had been heard in the village I slid down the scree until I reached the valley floor. I stopped in a grove of trees and listened, but not a sound broke the heavy silence. Casting around I found a track, leading, as I hoped, in the direction I wanted to go but all it did was to land me eventually amid a huge tumble of lava stone hills, gullies, boulders and stunted, dead trees.[4] For two more hours I stumbled on without seeing a living being. As the sun grew stronger the heat, reflected from the great boulders, became terrific. My throat was dry and my tongue felt like a lump of stone. Finally, when I was on the point of giving myself up for lost, I heard the distant bleat of a goat. Scrambling to the top of a hill I gave vent to the shepherd call of 'Oristo Ella', only to hear my voice mocked by the echoes. Lost I certainly was, but at least I could try to find some way out of this torrid wilderness. Struggling onwards, I rounded a small rise to make the joyful discovery of a herd of goats resting near a well. As I made my appearance a man armed with a rifle stepped from behind a boulder and spat a question at me in Greek. I told him eagerly that I was 'Austaloos' (an Australian), on hearing which he came forward and offered me a drink. Immediately, he was joined by four other Greeks, all of whom seemed disposed to be amiable. They permitted me to rest before detailing one of their number to show me a path that wound its erratic course in the direction of a settlement whose name, for important reasons, I cannot mention.[5]

From that point my journey might be said to have started again. It was one to remember, particularly that part of it which took me over hilltops crowned with a thorny bush about eight inches high. This plant grew so densely as to form a gigantic carpet, springy and beautiful to walk upon. Indeed, I was at peace with the world, and had made several hours' progress when, as though he had sprung from the earth, a figure rose up in front of me and threatened me with a shotgun. Wearing black, as most of these mountaineers did, and thrusting out his long, fierce beard this fellow was an awesome spectacle and caused me no end of a fright. As best I could I told him my story in his own language, informing him of my origin and of the destination I aimed to reach if I were not blown to pieces en route by one of the menacing guns which appeared to be so profuse in these parts. My pidgin-Greek was wasted upon him. The fellow spoke to me in raucous English! Not only did he speak, but he related, in detail, practically every episode of his career. He then allowed me to proceed unscathed.

Another two hours of hard walking brought me to the far edge of the plateau, and I realised that once I had made a descent from it I would once more be in dangerous territory.[6] There would inevitably be German patrols to dodge.

Far down in the valley, though avoiding villages, I met several Greeks to whom I passed myself off as German so as not to attract attention. At sundown, however, I came upon an old wood-gatherer making his way home. This simple, kindly man conducted me to his tiny house and put me into the care of his daughter who, when I had splashed my face and hands in icy water from the domestic well, prepared me a feast of beans boiled in oil—a feast which made a new man of me.

The wood-gatherer and I made our way, at our leisure, to the community nerve-centre—the local wine shop.[7] Here I listened to accounts of the doings of the Germans, parties of whom had only just completed a thorough search of the town. It seemed they were looking for Britishers. Apparently I had been lucky not to have appeared on the scene earlier.

10

IN GOOD COMPANY

A companionable Greek, at whose home I spent the night, refused to part with me until he had put me on the track and given me full directions as to which way to head. He was still giving me advice when we were joined by a band of bedraggled men carrying bundles. They were a party of Greek soldiers who had escaped from Albania,[1] and were now struggling back to their villages, which were in the general direction of my own destination. In spite of appearances they were splendid types and they offered no objection at all to the suggestion that I should temporarily become one of them. For my part, I found the arrangement a happy one, for they beguiled many a weary mile with tales of their exciting experiences.

By this time, the soles of my boots had worn through, but my new friends were more than equal to the emergency. Deftly and quickly they wove new soles from grape vines. But they were also so deft and quick on their own feet that I had difficulty in keeping up with them. At every village we were welcomed right royally, the band growing merrier and merrier after each stop, for they had a tremendous capacity for wine.

The country had improved marvellously and eventually we were moving through rich vegetation and among streams of crystal water. Nevertheless, I was destined to have a bad shock, for, on walking into a village square, we came face to face with a patrol of seven Germans. Fortunately, they showed no curiosity.

Less than a mile further on we descended into a valley in which I was astonished to see groups of New Zealand and

Australian troops lazing and yarning, with their rifles stacked against the trees. It was explained to me that they numbered about seventy, and were being fed by the local people. The Jerries never troubled them!

Leaving them to their leisure, we climbed upwards and onwards, successfully passing two enemy patrols, the second of which, however, questioned some of us in very poor Greek. Happily, I looked so much like a native that I was taken for one.[2]

When we jabbered, 'Ousie Anglichaise, alla poly Germania' ('No English, all plenty Germans') they let us proceed.

That night was spent in a creolie right in the centre of a village garrisoned by Austrians, some of whom we saw holding a drinking bout in the local wineshop. True, we did not dare enter the place in daylight, but after dark it proved quite safe.

The following day was agonising for me. As we plodded and stumbled over high ground overlooking the Mediterranean my feet began to perish under me. They were red raw, and even my ankles were bleeding. At every step I made a sloshy sound and suffered almost unendurable pain. It was obvious that I could not go on for long.

Having by-passed a lake in which a score or so of Germans were bathing,[3] we finally staggered into a village where my friends reluctantly decided to leave me until my feet healed. Handing me over to the ministrations of a wizened compatriot and his great fat wife, they all wrote out their addresses for me and bade me a sorrowful farewell. Words failed me when I tried to thank them for their kindness and protection. Indeed, no words would have sufficed.

When they had gone their way, my little host bathed my feet, fed me handsomely and took me to a hut outside the settlement. He told me I could sleep there without fear.

Later, two young lads came along with food and diverted me throughout the afternoon with their accounts of what the Germans had been doing. When they ultimately dragged themselves away I made a careful inspection of the locality with the object of spotting likely hiding-places. To the east, the plain was dotted with villages, large and small, and at no more than 200 yards distant from the hut there was a bitumen road.

Dusk was settling in when, attracted by the hum of aircraft, I discerned thirty enemy bombers out to sea, flying a few feet above the water.

It seemed quite like old times. Nor was I the only person interested, for practically every walking person in the village came out after dark to ask me whether the planes were 'Germania' or 'Englaishe'. It hurt me to tell them that they were enemy machines.

11

UP A TREE

Refreshed, I woke in the morning to be greeted by the little Cretan with a basket of freshly picked oranges. He asked me to give him my ragged and filthy clothes so his wife could wash and repair them. He left me alone and naked, promising to return in a few hours.

During the next morning I was the witness of a curious incident.

Glancing over the sea, so clear and blue in the early light, I saw two Nazi freighters of about 5,000 tons, each towing a barge, set a course for the Greek mainland. Though they departed so confidently without escort, it wasn't very long before they turned about and steamed back at full speed. Evidently these narrow waters had not proved as secure as they had expected. It cheered me to think that there might be some of our own ships out there, even now.

Early in the afternoon, when resting in a hut outside the village, I had the narrowest shave since my escape from the prison camp. Without warning a motor truck, crammed with Bulgarian soldiery, roared out of the silence and pulled up in the village. The troops, all of whom were armed with rifles, sprang from the vehicle. At a word of command from their officer, who brandished a Luger pistol, they fanned out preparatory to combing the neighbourhood.

There was no time for me to run; no time, in fact, to do more than swarm up the tree against which my shanty so miraculously had been built. The foliage offered some cover and I could only pray that I would not be seen. As two of the soldiers approached from different directions I pressed my body against the trunk, scarcely daring to breathe. One of the fellows stopped and aimed at the door of the hut while his companion advanced and peered inside. When he saw nothing of interest, he signed to his pal who at once came up and joined him under my tree, where they smoked and talked for almost fifteen minutes. It was perhaps the worst quarter of an hour of my life. The mere strain of keeping myself motionless was terrific. At length, however, a whistle summoned the two intruders back to the village and, to my great joy, I saw the entire party drive away. But I was so scared that I stayed up in those heaven-sent branches for a full hour.

I waited in my nakedness for my host to return with my clothes, but no one approached the hut. An hour before sunset I set out to beg or steal clothes and eventually met success in a lean-to behind an isolated house. The trousers were far too short in the legs and the tattered shirt did not meet across my chest but I was pleased to cover my nakedness.

Who informed the Germans I will never know.[1]

My one desire, now, was to leave this place before a trap was sprung. It was clearly dangerous to stay in one spot too long. Accordingly, after a night's rest, I made what I could of my suffering feet and took to the road again. It surprised me that my greetings to passers by were either ignored or regarded with suspicion. There were spies and informers everywhere. However, when struggling along a track between two small towns, I came upon a tattered Greeko panting under a huge bundle of brushwood.

'Kalimira Ducani,' ('Good morning, how are you?') I said.

I was answered with a slow smile.

'Englaishe?' he asked, softly.

I nodded.

He beckoned me to follow him and, leading me through some narrow village lanes, ushered me into a poor little house, spotlessly clean, but reeking with the smell of olive oil and garlic. No more than 200 yards down the lane twenty young Nazis, stripped to the waist but all carrying pistols, lay baking in the sun.

Somehow, their presence did not disturb me. I was pretty sure that no German could possibly recognise me as an Australian or anything else but an islander. I was dark enough from exposure to the sun, and hairy enough, by now, to be acknowledged as a true Cretan.

Two friends of my brushwood carrier popped in shortly after my entrance and one of them made me the magnificent gift of some tender tobacco leaves.[2]

At noon, feeling refreshed and not in the least afraid, I walked out with one of the Greeks and passed right by the basking Germans. As I had expected, they did not take the faintest notice of me.

I followed the path pointed out to me and stuck steadily to it until late in the afternoon. I had halted by a gushing water-course when two Cretans appeared from nowhere. Nothing was more remarkable than the way in which these people could materialise. However, this pair were perfectly friendly and could even converse in English. Once satisfied with my identity they showed me the local armoury. This had been very cleverly hidden and contained at least a hundred rifles of American, British, German and Greek types, as well as ample supplies of ammunition.

Talk veered, as it frequently did among the islanders, to the question of a possible revolution against the invaders. Revolution, in itself, presented no problem to the Greeks, who were accustomed to it in one form or another. But here, as elsewhere, action to evict the Germans was regarded with special zest. Apparently, however, there was little more than hope behind the present agitation.

After a mutual exchange of compliments I resumed my pilgrimage and quickly stumbled into rough lava-country afflicted with a vicious undergrowth of thorn bush. A lot of this was burning, with the result that when I was not being half choked with smoke I was skidding over bare, hot rocks.

It was late when I left the fire behind me and walked into

a village, where I proposed to rest for the night.[3] As usual, I did not have to search for a friend in need. A grey-bearded hunchback advanced upon me in the street and told me with humble kindness that I could spend some hours at his dwelling. There he introduced me to his daughter, a pretty girl dressed in European fashion and with such good taste that I was not surprised to learn that she and her father were French. I sat down to a splendid meal and some particularly good wine. A few Greeks subsequently joined our little party and until eleven o'clock we spent the time pleasantly in smoking and yarning. It was then agreed that I would be safer, after all, if I slept in a little cave they knew of just beyond the village. These good people were right. The cave proved quite tolerable and I was not disturbed.

Continuing my wanderings, I set my face towards the mountains and had gone a few miles when I struck a path winding through an olive grove on the edge of a plain. Here I came to a sharp halt, for in front of me were lines of British tents and a park of trucks, heavy motor cycles and trailers. Germans were moving busily throughout the camp, and scarcely 100 yards to the right of me a sentry was pacing slowly up and down.

Trying not to attract attention, I casually turned back into the grove and altered my course to the left, only to discover a second sentry patrolling a dump of oil barrels stacked amongst the trees. Once again, I retreated, this time pausing to pick a few olives, here and there, to allay suspicions.

Making a wide detour I plodded into the main street of a near-by village and brazenly mingled with a crowd of Greek civilians and German troops.[4] Convinced that none was especially interested in me, I sauntered to the outskirts and was on the point of negotiating the last straggling cottages when a Greek wished me good morning. 'Good morning,' I answered in his own language. Evidently I flattered myself upon my accent, for in a moment he was bawling at the top of his voice, 'English!' I took to my heels and kept running until the village had vanished behind a ridge.

In a little while I was squatting in a vineyard devouring grapes. Unfortunately, I was still tackling the first bunch when an angry voice roared cross the field. What was I to do? This might not only be discovery, but denouncement. I decided that I would be deaf and dumb.

The owner of the voice—and the vineyard—ran up to me, spitting curses to the full extent of his vocabulary. For five minutes he swore, raged and glared. Then, as if a thought had dawned in his head, he changed his tone. 'English!' he cried. Ceasing his vituperation, he grasped my hand and greeted me like a long-lost brother. Nothing would please him but that I should enter his hut and enjoy some real refreshment. With great pride he fed me with cucumber, bread and wine, and before letting me depart gave me minute directions as to the easiest and safest route to follow.[5]

12

A CIRCLE IS CLOSED

From a ridge, not far distant, I had a perfect view of the surrounding country. Still, the descent to the plain below took longer than I expected and several times I went astray, ending in some rocky gully. Thanks, however, to the guidance of shepherds I at last reached the road that led past the aerodrome where, some months before, I had been taken prisoner. I had completed the circle.

Heading for Retimo I passed through seven Nazi camps and a deal of German transport.[1] Then, within a mile of the town, I turned off and entered the torn vineyard which had seen the hardest of our fighting. Within sight was the blackened shell of the tank in which one of my mates, Mac[2], had been burnt alive. I felt the blood rising to my temples. Nothing seemed to have been touched. In front of me loomed a mound of dirt from which a decomposing arm stretched appealingly to the unresponsive heavens, and spread all over the field, sprawled where they had fallen, lay the bodies of those Australians whom I had seen die for what they believed right. They were so many awful shapes to which clothing clung by threads, and beside them were their rusty rifles. Not so much as a spadeful of earth had been spared them.

On leaving this ghostly place I struck along the familiar bitumen road, still pitted with shell holes. Heavy traffic forced me almost into the ditches. There were some careless drivers among those Germans!

Ahead of me was a cement bridge over a dry river course.

Here, judging by the long queue of vehicles, the Nazis had established an inspection post which, at all costs, I would have to avoid. I dived into a thick clump of bamboos, growing almost to the water's edge, and, once through these, skirted some farm buildings, still very pockmarked.[3] My objective, now, was the cottage of a Greek from whom, in far off days, we used to buy eggs.

Seeing me coming, the old chap poked his grizzled head out of his window and scowled ferociously. But I was not impressed. I leaned forward and whispered 'Australian'.

Instantly, the scowl gave place to a wrinkled smile and I was bidden to enter despite the fact that fifty Nazi troopers were billeted only a short distance away—so near, indeed, were they that we afterwards watched them lying about in the sunshine, some sheltering under umbrellas made from parachutes.

The dear old chap 'explained' me to his wife and daughter who immediately provided me with something to eat. I gained some inkling of the fervour of the anti-German feeling in the neighbourhood from my host's remark that whenever people walked past a German cemetery they would spit sideways to express their hate.

At sundown, I helped him to load some bedding upon his donkey and then all four of us started out for the nearest hills where, I was informed, groups of farmers would gather to protect their women from molestation. I had the happiness of being warmly greeted by some of these poor people.

I was awakened very early in the morning by the daughter who offered me a glass of warm goat's milk. All the other families had already left, so we wasted no time in getting back to the farm, where the son of the house, who had been absent for several days, was awaiting his parents. In his company I explored the old battlefield, being regaled at frequent intervals by his prolific curses upon the oppressors, for whom he did not seem to have blasphemy enough.

Giving the road a wide berth, we kept to the fields and peered into numerous slit trenches and bomb craters. In many of them were rusty food tins. Others had been caved in to form the grave of some unfortunate devil. The hill we had defended from the paratroops had its scars covered by a thick growth of grass and vines, but our old vineyard, I noticed, contained a crop of shiny black crosses, sown very close.[4] On the hilltop were the shattered remains of the field gun which had received a direct hit from a shell. It lay as a stark monument to the brave lads who had fought here and died unbroken in spirit. Afterwards, we wound our way down to a cool grove of olives beneath which many of my pals lay sleeping in eternal peace. The mounds appeared to be little changed since I had seen them last, except that some pious Greek women had placed a small cross of olive branches and a few flowers on each of them. I stood in the grove for a while and breathed a silent prayer.

We then made our way to the edge of the aerodrome which my companion told me warningly was forbidden territory. I was determined, however, to search for some Luger pistols which I had cached in the long-ago. Telling the lad to wait for me I left the cover of the olives and strode towards the airfield, well aware that I was tempting fate. I remembered the hiding place clearly. It was near a well, under some bushes. Though there were several Germans within a few yards, I walked straight to the cache, only to find that its contents had vanished. Picking up some branches, I nodded nonchalantly to the Jerries and went back the way I had come. They did not make a move to stop me.

Having spent another night in the hills, I said goodbye to the family and left richer than I had come. One Greek had given me a white silk shirt, another a pair of socks, and another a package of food as well as an old Luger and some ammunition.

Hours later, I stood on the far side of the mountain pondering which direction to take. Two roads lay before me. One led to Heraklion and the east, the other to the south.[5] I chose neither but instead began the ascent of a steep donkey path leading up a bush-covered ridge where, eventually, I found myself on a plateau. There was a village directly in front.[6] I resolved on the instant to rest in it for a few days, assuming that I would be 'adopted' in the customary way.

Not caring to intrude too soon, however, I bedded myself in the straw of a creolie and was in no time oblivious to the troubles of this world. The sun was high in the sky when a goat roused me from my slumbers by licking my face, but as this was not the sort of ablution I needed I walked to a house and was given permission to enjoy a real wash. Since, as I had expected, I was quickly made to feel at home in the village I repaid some of the kindness shown towards me by helping with the threshing in the fields and, like everybody else, used a large wooden pitchfork for the job.

Next day, I became a musician. I was induced to this artistry by the skill manifested by two male performers on bamboo flutes. The more they played the more I was intrigued. At last, I could restrain my enthusiasm no longer. I made myself an instrument just like theirs and fluted myself through the village as to the manner born.

Two old chaps, each obviously jealous of the other's importance, invited me to inspect their wines and decide who grew the better grapes.[7] I was only too willing to oblige, but as it turned out, the decision involved the eating of so many grapes during a period of several hours that the very thought of vineyards made my sensitive stomach sick for many a long day to come. Much to the disgust of the rivals I pronounced their wares exactly equal in quality!

13

PRIEST WITH A GUN

Day succeeded day, and it became hard to remember which it was. Monday meant no more to me than Wednesday. Nor was this strange, because I had already lost trace of weeks. However, a moment came when I realised it was Sunday. The tinkle of a church-bell brought the fact home to me. As no preacher lived in the village the inhabitants had to share the ministrations of one who lived in another settlement.

The service, on this occasion, did not begin until five o'clock in the afternoon, but the Sabbath was nevertheless observed as a day of rest. On the appearance of their 'Papa', who rode in on a tiny donkey draped with a scarlet rug, the worshippers crowded into their humble, whitewashed church. They were all dressed in their best and brightest.

Reluctant to intrude and being unfamiliar with the rites of the Greek Orthodox Church, I watched the service through an open window. It was impressive and touching, and I especially liked the singing of the hymns, which echoed so beautifully in the still air.

Afterwards, I wandered into a house to which I had been bidden for the evening meal, and to my astonishment was soon followed there by the priest and two well-dressed Greeks,[1] all three of whom looked me over keenly. Addressing me in English, with an authentic Oxford accent, the priest asked me my name and where I came from. When I told him, he removed his long black cloak and sat down. In his belt were two heavy revolvers!

Had I, he asked, anything by which I could identify myself?

I had to admit that I hadn't. I had destroyed my military papers, I explained, because I feared that I might be recaptured. I mentioned, however, that I still had a few photographs of sentimental value.

Had I ever been to England?

I replied that I had. Other questions, a dozen at least, followed in quick succession, and I was able to answer them convincingly.

Then came the big surprise.

'Would you like to be in Alexandria in a number of days?' he asked.

For a moment I was taken aback. I could scarcely believe my ears.

'Yes,' I said emphatically.

That night, escorted by the priest's two companions,[2] I left the village and walked for several hours until, at last, from a distant ridge, I looked down upon a beautiful village glistening in the moonlight—a village like no other that I had yet seen.[3] Hazy with thoughts of my wonderful good fortune, I glanced dazedly at my protectors, who, offering no comment, led me down and then through a courtyard into a house. The room to which I was conducted was well furnished, and without delay I was supplied with sweet bread and wine. Later, the elder of my two guardians presented me with a pair of good quality riding breeches and a fine shirt. I felt like a millionaire. Then, each smoking a cigarette, we slipped out and made ourselves comfortable in a vineyard, sleeping cosily in rugs brought from the house.

A somewhat embarrassing ceremony awaited me in the morning. It was quite clear, when I was conducted indoors again, that I was an object of curiosity and a subject of excited conversation. Quite a crowd of people came in to inspect me. Well, I had no objection to that. But when the attractive niece of one of my escorts made me a speech of welcome and then proceeded to wash my face and hands as though I were a baby, I felt considerably upset. However, it was an old Cretan custom and I had to make the best of it.[4]

That I was a popular figure in the village was evident from the hospitality that was showered upon me in every quarter. I was obliged to drink innumerable toasts and eat far more than was good for me. Kindness, you might say, peeped from every corner.

Towards noon on the second day a German patrol arrived in the village, which I was told had been classified by the enemy as 'friendly'. Little did the nine men of that patrol know that while they rested from the heat and refreshed themselves they were 'covered' all the time by twenty well-armed Greekos who, at the first sign of trouble, would have shot them dead.

When the intruders had departed the life of the community went on as usual. I was given a haircut by a dapper little barber from Athens and spent several hours in gossiping. The villagers took advantage of the evening moonlight to gather on their balconies and talk incessantly of their hopes and fears, of the English, the Germans and the Russians, until it was time to go to bed.[5]

Next day, as the measure of their trust, I was taken by some of these friendly citizens to a fertile valley on the other side of the hills. Here, in an orange grove, a profusion of arms was concealed. Before sunset we had cleaned and put into working order fully 200 rifles.[6]

Back 'home' again I was told that a feast had been organised and that fifty guests, some of whom had come considerable distances, were to be present. There was to be an honoured place for me.[7]

A Greek official presided at the table and there was much to eat and drink. I confess I baulked when snails, baked in olive oil, were offered to me as one of the 'courses'.[8] For politeness' sake I mastered the tricky technique of removing a slug from the shell with a fork and, to my surprise, found it quite tasty. But this one was enough.

At the appointed time, eager though I was to reach the coast, I left the village with a heavy heart. There were some who tried to persuade me to marry one of the local girls and 'settle down' as the leader of a band of guerillas, but I was not tempted. My whole desire was to get back to Egypt as quickly as possible. But there was a lot of weeping when I said goodbye, and truth to tell, I was not far from tears myself.

14

FUGITIVES FOREGATHER

My guides piloted me through many villages until, on the second day, having coped with a stretch of bad country, we stopped at a straggling hamlet[1] where a portly, grey-headed elder greeted us in fluent English.[2] His linguistic skill, he explained, had been acquired during service with the British Navy in the last war. He added, with an air of pride, that he 'had' twenty or more New Zealand soldiers and two English officers in hiding. Like me, they were waiting for a chance to 'get off' but when that would be, he could not say. Perhaps in a week, perhaps longer, perhaps sooner.

Two Kiwis, who appeared on the scene, agreed with him. They had been directed here by various underground routes but they were of the opinion that it would be hopeless to leave until the moon had waned a week hence. I gathered that another bunch of New Zealanders and Australians had escaped from the island from here during the previous month.

Later in the day I met most of the other fugitives and found the tales of their experiences as interesting as they found mine.

The countryside proved a veritable Eden, for not only were we free to eat as we wished but there were caves in all directions into which we could disappear if danger threatened. What with swimming, sunbaking and reaching for grapes and figs as they grew, the hours went like a dream. Of course, we were more or less in rags and must have looked like outlaws, but our hearts were light, particularly as we had complete faith in the loyalty of every farmer and villager. We trusted their intelligence service, too.

For example, on 9 August they received advance news of the
approach of a large German patrol. We were instantly shown
to a big cave and warned on no account to make a noise. So
long as we lay low and kept complete silence, they would do
the rest.

The cave was as hot as Hades, and we had neither water nor
food. Moreover, the patrol was not content with searching the
village. It settled down to take its ease. Hot and hungry, we
cursed those Nazis with every word we had.

Incidentally, I noticed that the two officers among us, a
captain and a lieutenant of Commandos, did not get along very
well with the lesser fry. The Kiwis believed they were bribing
the Greekos for extra food and tobacco. Anyhow, the pair always
seemed to have smokes when at best we had only one cigarette
to every four or five men.

One hefty New Zealander used to express his opinion aloud.
'Hey Joe,' he would say to one of the officers, 'give's a bloody
smoke!'

Like everything else the day came to an end, and on getting
the right word we trooped through the cool evening air to the
village. My host compensated me for the ordeal of the cave by
plying me with almond gin and krassy. Needless to say, the world
was soon a rosier place to live in.

Next day we were allowed to visit our accustomed swimming
pool, where, for a change, we staged a real carnival. Literally
for hours, we dived, swam and basked. Not until nearly dusk
did we wind ourselves back up the path straight into the blood-
red rays of the setting sun.

The village was seething with panic. It seemed that a
shepherd on one of the neighbouring hills had seen a German
spying through binoculars.[3] Already, some of the Greeks had
fled, and it was plain to see that those who remained were
frightened. Men were arguing and women were wailing.
Everybody, indeed, took it for granted that the Germans would
come out in force and massacre the entire population.

Obviously, it was time for us to make ourselves scarce if only
out of consideration for our benefactors. Bolting a meal, we
took a long walk to the top of a mountain where our guide

promised to return to us on the morrow. In spite of the rugs and water with which we had been supplied, we spent a very cold and uncomfortable night.

As the sun rose, however, we began to hanker after that coldness. We grilled and simmered in the burning heat and the rocks under us were like hot coals. Yet, from this lofty quoin, our eyes could sweep over a wide arc of the Mediterranean. For us, it glistened as the Sea of Deliverance, but it was still a great barrier between us and liberty. Between us and escape lay those 280 miles of hungry blue water. And, talking of water, we were sadly in need of a drink. Long before noon our jar was empty, and for the remainder of that torrid day we thirsted with parched throats.

Not until an hour after nightfall did the rattling of loose stones proclaim the return of our faithful Greekos who were doubly welcome because they had had the good sense to bring food and drink with them. They had been unable to come sooner because the Germans had returned and made a fresh search of the village. The general position was so unsatisfactory that we were advised to change our hide-out. Since we never disputed the wisdom of our good angels we followed them to another cave and settled down for the night. This time, in addition to stuffiness, we had to put up with the aroma of goats.

The next day was very much like the last, except that the boys seemed more disposed to cheer themselves up by discussing what they would do when they got to Alexandria. What letters they would write! What dinners they would eat! What beer they would drink!

When, as usual, our water gave out, another fellow and I decided to carry the jar down to a creek, which trickled along some 2,000 feet below. It was no light walk, but we rewarded ourselves with a dip in the deliciously cool water. On coming out, however, we were startled to see the fresh imprint of a German boot in the soft sand. Undoubtedly it was time to be off. Though the climb was a stiff one we did not dally about it and thought ourselves lucky to arrive back, complete with jar, without having a patrol at our heels.

Again our Greek comrades insisted, that night, that we should seek another cave. Again, we were destined to spend a grilling day in the hills. But this time the monotony was broken by the advent of four more New Zealanders, whose enthusiasm raised our spirits to a new high. They told us that a few days earlier a priest had whispered the magic words which we had already heard and that they had made for the rendezvous at top speed, armed, to our great satisfaction, with a supply of tobacco leaves. The things these lads had to tell us kept us interested for hours. Still, we were not sorry when, at sunset, the Greekos appeared with the welcome news that we could now return in safety to our comfortable creolies. Henceforth, there were days of peace and contentment, especially for me. As the only Australian on the scene I was the special favourite of the inhabitants who vied with each other in trying to make me feel at home. Every door was open to me; I was bidden to every table. There was no end to the generosity shown towards me.

August 16th, I remember, was a gala day, for after spending halcyon hours in our swimming pool we were all invited to a party. It was an occasion that will always live in my memory. We ate fowls roasted in butter, we drank our fill of wine, we smoked and we joined in the gaiety, the simple gaiety of these honest, homely people. In the intervals of retelling all the local gossip and rumours, the Greekos sang and danced to the music of flutes. Most of the rumours were of Allied victories concerning which we were frankly sceptical. Our Greek friends, however, absolutely believed in them. The wish, perhaps, was father to the thought.

The moon had waned a lot by now and the boys were becoming impatient. At a conference on 19 August it was resolved to send two delegates to the village headman to inquire what the prospects were. We had to make up our minds whether it would be better to wait where we were or push on to another likely spot. However, before we could take any action an Australian major and a strange Greek walked in on us. The officer confided that he was in touch with the British Secret Service and expected good news in the very near future. His object in coming amongst us was to discover how many we were.

Altogether, he talked so optimistically that our fears and doubts were put at rest. We were our bright selves again. As a parting shot the major assured us that he would keep in touch and let us know the moment when anything was 'doing'. In the circumstances, the two appointed delegates had a sinecure.

If you had searched the world, I don't suppose you could have seen anything more ludicrous than the appearance of some of our New Zealanders. Their sartorial styles were many and weird, dating down through the years to the naughty 'nineties. Several strutted about in straw college hats cocked well over the eye; another sported a bowler hat which he seemed to regard as a halo to his long beard; a few wore caps of strange shape; and there were two Kiwis walking round in ancient Turkish costume, turban, shirt, droopy-bottomed trousers and leather knee-boots complete. And, of course, everybody carried a walking-stick in the Greek fashion.

This was the motley lot who, within two days of the major's visit, was sent flying helter-skelter to the goats' cave by a report that a German patrol was on the way. Probably no more fantastic procession had ever been seen in those hills.

Fortunately, the alarm was brief. By next day we were back at the village.

15

'WE MOVE TONIGHT'

The news we had been waiting for, and almost despaired of, came on 22 August. Hot-foot from our Secret Service acquaintance came a messenger to say that we were to move to the coast on the following night. Such was the excitement that we could talk of nothing else. We were as happy as sandboys until we heard from our Greek friends that the Germans had unexpectedly caught four Australians and New Zealanders en route to the village, and instead of taking them prisoners had lined them up and shot them to pieces, there and then.

Our spirits, which had been so high, sank to the depths. All we could think of was revenge. One of the officers—the captain—tactlessly remarked the 'fools' must have been careless. Before he could speak another word, a Kiwi had smashed him to the ground. It served him right!

Slowly, slowly the hours came and went. All through the next day—and a blistering one it was—we were perpetually asking the time of the only man amongst us who possessed a watch. Every hour was like a week; every minute like a day. As I lay on the stones of the cave I tried to picture to myself just what freedom would be like. And what, I asked myself, would be the outcome of our great adventure?

As the shadows of evening lengthened a band of faithful Greeks came to wish us God's speed and to leave two of their number to guide us to the seashore. The Greeks produced wine and drank to our success with the tears falling shamelessly down their rough cheeks.

Then, when the last adieus had been spoken, we were led along precipitous goat tracks, down steep gravel slides, up winding country paths and over fields to a tree-lined stream on a distant plain. Here we could smell the sea and, in a short time, hear it. The sneering moon no longer held sway in the sky. We marched in pitch darkness. Indeed, it was so black that we kept bumping into one another.

Yet, something darker than the night loomed suddenly ahead, and there came a tense whisper from those in front, 'Jerries along the track a bit. Scatter in the bush and keep bloody quiet.'

An aching pain gripped my heart. To leave that track was like losing all hope of life.

I found a boulder and threw myself down behind it, too disappointed to care whether or not it was good cover. In this bleak place we stayed until dawn, when one of the chaps crept over and told me to follow him back to a hill which would provide better hiding.

Afterwards, the Commando captain explained the reason for our failure.[1] One of the guides, he said, had gone forward of the party and had contacted a strong German patrol waiting on the path to the beach. If it had not been for this, we should have been dead men—or prisoners. However, we were to make a fresh attempt that night.

Towards noon we were reinforced by two Australians who had many hair-rising tales to narrate. And the Greekos, thoughtful to the end, sent up two priests laden with evil-smelling cheese and brown bread. The cheese, unfortunately, was 'alive'.

Queer though it may seem, the Germans seemed to have a healthy respect for the long-haired, black-gowned Cretan priesthood, possibly because of the extraordinary influence they wielded over the population. The word of a priest had more 'law' to it than all the cruelty and suffering enforced by the hated invaders.

At half an hour before sunset a guide appeared and spoke for some minutes to the Commando captain. The latter drew us into a circle and gave us our orders.

Waiting for complete darkness we stole down the hill in parties of eight so that if the Germans were on the warpath there would be at least a chance of the majority of us evading capture. We walked for half an hour before coming to a halt, and scattering from the track. A couple of minutes later a low whistle brought us back. The pause, we discovered, had been made necessary by the appearance on the track of a group of British soldiers approaching from a neighbouring village.

In no time we stood on the edge of a cliff and looked down upon a small bay of choppy water.[2] The bay could not have been more than 150 yards wide at the mouth, narrowing to a stretch of sand merely 20 yards in length. A narrow goat track meandered down the cliff face and its footholds were so precarious that our descent was slow and dangerous. Finally, however, we stood, or rather, crouched, on the sand, pressing our bodies against the rock at the base. We were instructed to remain absolutely still and not to open our mouths. The reason for this order was soon obvious. The rays of a searchlight suddenly stabbed from one of the headlands and swept the sea

A recent view of Limni, which was used by submarines to evacuate British escapees from Crete in 1941.

and shoreline in a wide arc. For two full minutes it played over the area and then, once more, the night went black.

Gradually more and more men slithered to the beach while we held our breath and prayed that the searchlight would not reveal what was going on. Soon, there was quite a crowd on the sands, including a number of Greeks.

The action we were pining for came with a whispered message, passed from mouth to mouth, that we were to swim. Piece by piece we stripped ourselves of clothing, each article being whisked away by a Greek as it was removed.[3] Still there was no command to enter the water. When an hour passed we began to curse ourselves for having parted with our clothes, for the wind played havoc with our nakedness.

'There it is,' whispered some optimist, pointing out to sea, but we looked in vain for 'it' and did not know, in any case, what 'it' was likely to be.

We were virtually half dead with cold and suspense and I was beginning to feel that I could stand no more when a figure with a rope tied round his waist emerged from the water.[4] One of the men on the beach met him and addressed him in tones of authority, whereupon the sailor—for that is what he was— made the rope fast to a boulder. The man who had spoken to him then waded into the sea and began swimming. When next we saw him, in ten minutes or so, he had returned with a canvas boat about ten feet long. The senior man from each village was told to report to him and at a hurried conference the order of departure was settled, our own group being the last. Two wounded men were placed in the boat and ferried out to sea and after that the remainder of those on the beach took to the water at intervals of 20 seconds. The eyes of those who waited their turn were glued upon the searchlight station in dread that it would spring to life again. When there were only five men in front of me I stamped with fierce impatience. It seemed that they would never move, Four, three, two, one—I dived and began to swim, reaching for the rope. I could not find it. I could scarcely see a yard in any direction. But I kept on swimming. Some eighty yards from the shore I heard someone thrashing about to my left. Turning towards the thrasher I glimpsed the shadow of a face and a pair of hands. I discovered that the owner of these features was a Greeko and that he had the rope in his grasp.[5] Little by little I struggled on until I sighted a long black shape low in the water, heaving in the swell. It was a submarine.[6]

With joy and relief I swam alongside, only to find that her sloping deck was five feet above the waterline and slippery with grease. It was impossible to heave myself aboard, so I started to swim towards the stern, half in panic lest she should submerge before I could get a footing. Round the stern I went, and then as far as the bow. Nowhere could I see any way of climbing on deck. At last, in sheer desperation, I gave vent to a low cry and commenced to tread water. Even then, there was no sign that I had been seen or heard. So, without any thought of anything except my own need of rescue, I yelled for help. Almost immediately a rope hit the water near my head. I grabbed it tightly and was pulled over the side by a man stripped to the waist. At once I was led towards the conning tower where two sailors, sitting on the hatch, demanded my number, rank, name and regiment.

Once inside, a dozen cigarettes were thrust into my eager hands, and I was free to look about in the dim light. The ship was terrifically crowded. Naked men, coated with oil and grease, sprawled everywhere. They all wore an expression of deep contentment and were smoking avidly. Every now and again members of the crew dashed through the mob on their various duties. Joining a group who were in conversation with one of the sailors I heard that the submarine had taken 101 men aboard, and that these, plus 86 of the crew, constituted a record. Evidently, the captain was rather dubious about the weight of this load of humanity. And small wonder!

The thought that some of us might be jettisoned, as it were, did not enter my head. All I was conscious of as I dreamed away into a sleep of exhaustion was the noise of the engines starting.

Four days later—28 August—the sub safely glided into Alexandria. It was something almost too incredible to realise.

During the run across food had been severely rationed, but after our long course of olive oil dishes and odd scraps, we felt we were living in luxury.

When the hatch was opened to admit the blinding sunshine it was as though we had been given a glimpse of paradise. We crowded up the ladder and gazed round the harbour with singing hearts.

The light-spirited, laughing crew of the mother ship to which we tied up were a reminder, however, that we were still of this world. Slowly we scrambled to the deck of the larger vessel—a procession of gaunt, naked and bearded apparitions as little like our original selves as could be imagined. Loudly those British tars cheered us. Friendly and man-to-man was their welcome. But the most touching moment of all was when the men of the submarine, our saviours, also sent us a cheer.

The same sun that had burned down on us in Crete shone over us now. It was, I told myself, beating down, at this very moment, on the hills and plains over which I had travelled for so many weary months. I prayed that it would soon shine upon those brave islanders, so self-sacrificing and hardy, on a day of freedom such as we,[7] who owed so much to them, now enjoyed.[8]

Lew Lind (left) with two men from his regiment soon after his return from Crete.

APPENDIX:
THE BATTLE FOR CRETE, 1941

An address delivered by Lew Lind to The Naval Historical Society
of Australia, 3 September 1971

The Prelude

The Battle of Crete will be remembered in history because it was the
first and probably the last truly airborne battle ever waged. It was
won and lost by the most perplexing mistakes on both sides.

The prelude to the battle commenced in October 1940, when the
British decided to establish a naval base at Suda Bay. The 160-mile
island occupied a similar position in the eastern Mediterranean as
Malta did in the west. In addition to providing an advanced base for
Admiral Cunningham's Fleet, it provided a convenient air base for
bombing the vital Romanian oilfields on which Germany depended.
Lastly, the island separated Italy from its bases in the Dodecanese
Islands. By December 1940, the seven-mile long harbour of Suda Bay
was developed for a naval base. A squadron of Walrus amphibians
operated from the bay and a British garrison strengthened the small
Greek Army.

Italy struck the first blow of the battle that same month. Bombers
from nearby Scarpanto commenced regular raids on the base.
However, the first months of 1941 saw Italy facing defeat on three
fronts: Graziano was hurled back in Libya, the British forces in
Ethiopia and Somaliland were advancing, and in Albania the Greek
Army was forcing the Italians out of the mountains and down to the
sea.

In March 1941, Hitler ordered his armies to turn south and stabilise
the situation. At the same time British and Anzac troops entered
Greece. Rommel also landed his Afrika Korps in Tripoli.

The Greek Campaign lasted a little over three weeks. The British
Forces, outnumbered ten to one, fought a clever rearguard action and
at the end of the month were successfully evacuated by the Royal Navy.

March also saw the first naval action in the Crete campaign. It
was a brilliant stroke by the famous Italian 10th Light Flotilla. Six
EMBs (explosive motor boats) under the command of Lieutenant
Faggioni, attacked British shipping in Suda Bay. The tiny plywood

boats roared into Suda Bay, skipped over the anti-submarine net and began a seven-mile suicidal run down the bay to the anchorage. All ships opened fire on the elusive targets and four were knocked out before they could attack. The remaining two raced in among the anchored shipping and carefully selected the two largest targets. Two hundred yards from their goal the EMB pilots locked the steering of their craft and dived overboard. The first boat crashed into the side of Cunningham's only 8-inch cruiser, *York*, and exploded with a deafening roar. The second boat homed on the 10,000-ton tanker *Pericles*. *York* sank within minutes in water so shallow the cruiser rested on the bottom with her decks dry. *Pericles*, on fire and with a great hole in her hull, was beached.

Ten thousand troops evacuated from Greece were landed in Crete. These were mainly elements of the 6th Australian Division and the New Zealand Division. During the early days of May they were strengthened by the 2,000-strong Royal Marine Mobile Naval Base Defence Organisation, 1st Welsh, 2nd Yorks and Lancs, and the 2nd Black Watch. General Bernard Freyberg of New Zealand Division was appointed commander of this force and became responsible for the defence of the island. The tall ex-Royal Marine had won a Victoria Cross at Gallipoli in 1915 when, as a junior lieutenant, he swam ashore before the landing and placed beacons on the various beaches.

It was an unenviable command. Although the forces at Freyberg's disposal appeared impressive on paper, in reality they were weak. The Australian and New Zealand units were well below strength and all heavy weapons had been destroyed on the beaches in Greece. There was no artillery except thirty old Italian field pieces lacking instruments and some 3.7 and light Bofors ack-ack guns. His armour consisted of six worn-out and damanged 'I' tanks and a similar number of light scouting tanks. Air support was six Hurricanes and seventeen Gloster-Gladiator biplanes.

Freyberg prepared his defences well. The island's three small airstrips, Maleme, Retimo and Heraklion, were to be defended against air assault. Beaches at Georgiopolous, Suda Bay and Canea were garrisoned to resist a sea assault.

Hitler had approved the assault on Crete on Anzac Day while the Battle of Kriekuri was in full swing. Command was given to the elated General Student, who was eager to launch his airborne army into a battle which would be their exclusive domain.

However, supplies soon became a problem on both sides. The German airborne troops were in Germany, but the aircraft were scattered all over Occupied Europe. Communications from Germany to Greece were primitive. Because of the inability to transport troops, equipment and stores to the start point the invasion was postponed from 16 to 20 May.

The British were in even greater difficulties. Freyberg had been promised 30,000 tones of stores in the month, but by 2 May the Luftwaffe was attacking Suda Bay and within a fortnight it was completely unusable by day. From then on supplies had to be brought in by night by warships, and when the battle began on 20 May only 3,000 of the 30,000 tons promised had arrived. One of the omissions in this cargo were 25-pounder guns which would have turned the battle in the British favour. Although over 100 were available in Alexandria, the Army command sent a batch of worthless captured Italian guns. Fifty of those 25-pounders would have won the battle.

Air Fleet IV, under the general command of General Lohr, was allocated to the task of taking the island. The Air Fleet consisted of 1,330 aircraft including 600 Junkers troop carriers, 280 bombers, 150 Stukas, 200 fighters and 60 reconnaissance aircraft. To this may be added 80 gliders. A force of 22,750 men was available, drawn from 7th Airlanding Division and 22nd Airborne Division. The latter were in reserve and their place in the battle was taken by 5th and 6th Mountain Divisions and 5th Armoured Division.

Freyberg concentrated his strength in this order: at Maleme, New Zealand Division supported by Royal Marines, 1st Welsh and two Australian battalions (10,000 men); at Heraklion, 2nd Black Watch, 2nd Leicesters, 2/4th Battalion of Australians (4,000 men); and at Retimo, 2/1st and 2/11th Battalions and support troops (1,200 men). Another 5,000 men were stationed at Georgiopolous, Suda Bay and Canea.

The German bombing of the port and airstrips intensified from 15 May. On the 18th, the British Air Force in Crete ceased to exist. Outnumbered twenty to one and outclassed, they were in a hopeless position.

At Retimo, where I was stationed, a flight of six Gladiators, manned by American volunteers, took to the air as opportunity offered. This was usually when the enemy air strength in the immediate vicinity had dropped below double figures. On 18 May two Gladiators remained. They took off against a force of forty Messerschmitts and Heinkels. Both planes succeeded in downing an enemy before plummetting into the sea.

Despite lack of guns, tanks and transport, Freyberg had prepared his positions well. The main troops were skilfully dug in to cover the three aerodromes. Camouflage was superlative. Despite continuous reconnaissance, the presence of spies and a fifth column, the Germans remained ignorant of the defences until they landed.

At Retimo a reconnaissance plane was shot down by rifle fire on 18 May. A detailed map salvaged from the wreck showed only five infantry posts of 150 correctly marked.

The Assault Begins

The battle named Operation Scorcher by Churchill and Operation Merkur by the Germans, opened at 6.30 a.m. on 20 May. The defenders were waiting in their gun pits and foxholes. 'Stand to' had been ordered at 4.30 a.m. The first indication was a continuous roar of aircraft engines echoing across the sea from the north. The massed strength of General Lohr's Air Fleet IV, 1,330 aircraft, was on its way to Crete.

Two hundred and forty bombers, dive-bombers and fighters unleashed a rain of bombs and bullets on Maleme and the area east of Canea. For ninety minutes the air trembled to the never-ending crash of bombs and the roar of machine-guns and cannon.

At 7.50 a.m. another aircraft armada estimated to be more than 400 aircraft (250 Junkers 52 transports, 60 gliders and 150 fighters and bombers) crossed the coast near Retimo. They turned east and converged on Maleme like a plague of locusts. As the air fleet came in sight the only air resistance to the invasion met it. A single Fleet Air Arm Fulmar, which had lost its carrier and landed at Maleme, took off and dived into the leading ranks of the German transports. It shot down two Junkers before it went down under a withering fire from the escorting fighters.

The transports levelled off at 250 feet and as they ran in over the target they spewed out a fountain of multi-coloured parachutes. The Storm Regiment of 7th Airborne Division had commenced its assault.

Immediately they were greeted by the fire of the New Zealanders waiting below. Bodies jerked beneath their parachutes. The defenders learnt quickly. Instead of firing at individual parachutists, they concentrated their fire on the jump hatches. The Germans were in strings of fifteen attached to a static line, and when the first man was hit he invariably dragged his fourteen companions out with him. When this happened the parachutes failed to open and the whole string crashed to earth.

In the heat of this fantastic battle the silent descent of the sixty black-painted gliders passed almost unnoticed. Organised in Staffels of fifteen gliders, with a total of 135 men to a Staffel, they landed in the lightly defended Tavrionitas River, a dry river bed strewn with boulders four feet in diameter. Over one-third of the gliders struck the boulders at sixty miles per hour and their crews were killed instantly. The survivors, however, although under fire from air force ground crew and a company of New Zealanders, were able to organise in dead ground.

The first wave of parachutists were shot or bayonetted if they landed alive. A second armada followed but they dropped on the fringe of the defences. A third was dropped in a valley between Maleme and Canea. When the last Germans reached the ground the fighters and bombers returned, but they were helpless. It was impossible to identify friend from foe.

Communications with the other strongholds at Heraklion and Retimo failed soon after the attack. Lieutenant-Colonel Campbell in command at Retimo rightly guessed a landing had been made at Maleme. Brigadier Chappel at Heraklion had no knowledge of the attack until 3 p.m.

At 3.30 p.m. the Heraklion defences were attacked by a force of over 200 bombers and fighters. Although the defenders were well equipped with ack-ack guns, not a round was fired at the low-flying planes. In consequence, their positions were not revealed. Chappel's 4,000 troops were well dug in and casualties from the attack were negligible. At 4.15 p.m. the bombers and fighters withdrew and a deadly silence settled on the dust-enshrouded area.

Ten minutes later came the roar of the assault armada flying in from the north. The Junkers 52s came in at about 250 feet and as they crossed the coast they banked sharply and swung east to approach the airfield. Dug in around the airstrip were the 2nd Black Watch Battalion. The 2nd Leicesters were in position about half a mile south-west of the airstrip, and in front of them on two conical hills called 'the Charlies' was the Australian 2/4th Battalion.

Immediately before the first paratrooper jumped a bugler of the Black Watch sounded the general alarm. The notes drifted across the airstrip as hell broke loose.

The ack-ack guns opened up at point blank range. The lead plane in the formation was hit, it side-slipped with flames pouring from its engines and exploded between the Charlies. Eight others followed, carrying their human cargoes to a violent end.

Parachutists were floating down right on top of the Black Watch. As the battalion diary recorded, 'Every soldier picked his swaying target and fired and picked another one and fired again'. When the first wave were on the ground the troops moved in with the bayonets. Behind the Black Watch, the Australian 2/4th Battalion accounted for the overs.

The German timetable had gone haywire. Delays in aircraft returning to their fields and slow loading resulted in the 2,000 paratroopers intended for Heraklion being despatched in a series of small waves. It was not until 7.30 p.m., three hours after the assault began, that the last drop was made. The interval between the drops allowed the defenders to deal effectively with each group. Within an hour the Black Watch killed 300 men and 12 officers in their sector, and wounded 100 men and 8 officers. The other battalions reported similar results.

The German force dropped at Heraklion was I Parachute Regiment and a Battalion of II Parachute Regiment, all under the command of Colonel Brauer. Before the night was over, 1,000 of Colonel Brauer's 2,000 picked men were dead.

At the same time the assault was made on Heraklion, a force of 2,000 paratroopers from 2 Parachute Rifle Regiment and 3 Parachute Battalion, under Colonel Sturm, attacked Retimo.

The weakest held of the three airstrips, Retimo was defended by two depleted Australian battalions, 2/1st and 2/11th, and six guns of doubtful efficiency, all under the command of Lieutenant-Colonel Ian Campbell.

I was at Retimo and I should add that not all the 1,500 defenders had rifles. There were four Bren guns to each battalion, four mortars and eighty bombs, and two boxes of grenades. There were two medical officers and their equipment was carried in their small haversacks. The force had food for two days. I have given these details because at Retimo was won the only British victory in Crete.

The airstrip was about four miles west of the town, a dusty strip between two small hills. These were labelled Hill A, 2/1st Battalion, and Hill B, 2/11th Battalion. The infantry were dug in on the slopes of the hills and the artillery on the crowns.

A force of 150 bombers and fighters opened up the attack at 3.30 p.m. They bombed and strafed erratically as they had no accurate information on the defence positions. At 4.15 p.m. they departed and headed back to their aerodromes. The total result of their attack was one donkey killed. Ten minutes later the transports arrived. The first assault was made by 240 planes. The paratroopers were dropped from about 200 feet in strings of fifteen.

The following is quoted from *The Battle of Retimo:, The Unofficial History of 2/3rd Field Regiment*.

The gunners in their pits stiffened as they saw the paratroopers, legs apart and braced, standing poised in the open doorways. Suddenly the sky was filled with diving bodies, blossoming parachutes and an endless cavalcade of planes. As each Junker reached the dropping zone another cloud of parachutes appeared. At first we were not aware of the spray of bullets striking the ground around us.

'Look out,' somebody yelled. 'They're shooting at us.'

The first wave landed on the defences of 2/1st Battalion on Hill A: 'The 2/1st opened up from all sides. Bodies danced in the air as they were struck by a fusillade of bullets. Some reached the ground only to be blasted off their feet.' Those who did land unhurt were often bayonetted as they struggled to free themselves from their harnesses.

On the crown of the hill the gunners were unarmed except for their doubtful field pieces and one rifle. Again quoting from *The Battle of Retimo*:

Almost immediately a tall paratrooper, grim in his flapping jump suit, burst into the open and sprayed the gun pit with his Tommy gun. He bounded forward and they swung their 100 mm field gun around. When the German was 10 feet away they fired point blank. The shell struck the man at chest level and he vanished in a puff of flame and smoke.

A ferocious battle of hide-and-seek developed in the olive groves and vineyards. Bayonets stabbed and Tommy guns stuttered in a deadly game of kill or be killed. The chatter of guns and the crump of grenades was broken only by the cries of the wounded.

The second wave of paratroopers fell on Retimo at 5 p.m., landing on Hill B where the West Australians of 2/11th Battalion waited. Another slaughter began. Close to 400 Germans landed in a vineyard 150 feet by 100 feet. Here developed a ferocious battle that continued until darkness.

When night fell on Retimo 400 dead Germans and 100 dead Australians lay in an area of three acres.

A different type of battle was waged in the dark, as the Australians began stalking the Germans. The silence was broken by a scream or a torrent of fire.

On Hill A the Germans had driven the defences back from the airstrip and up the hill to the ridge. The Australians were outnumbered. On Hill B the Germans were given no chance to assemble. They were hunted relentlessly.

At Maleme, when night fell, the first blunder was committed on the hill dominating the aerodrome. Lieutenant-Colonel Andrews, commanding the New Zealand 22nd Battalion, ordered his men to fall back from Hill 107, which was the key to the battle. Because of disrupted communications he had lost contact with his forward companies and believed, erroneously, that these troops had been wiped out. In fact, the forward companies were intact and the Germans were in a perilous condition. Their casualties were so high that not even one company remained intact.

At midnight, Hill 107 was evacuated and surprised paratroopers occupied it. At that moment the battle was lost. The Germans had possession of an aerodrome.

The night of 20 May was agonising for both General Student and General Freyberg. In his headquarters in the Hotel Grande Bretagne in Athens, Student was admitting defeat. The reports received from Maleme and Heraklion told of shocking casualties. From Retimo there had been complete silence and this silence was to remain throughout the campaign. Student wrestled with the decision of evacuation and just before dawn he decided to send one of his staff, Captain Kleye, to Maleme and return with an assessment of the situation. Kleye landed just after dawn, in dead ground on the edge of the airstrip, and minutes later he was flying back to Athens with the news it was possible to land at Maleme. An hour later the first six Junkers 52s landed reinforcements. From then onwards a shuttle service ran between the Greek aerodromes and Maleme.

The Navy Pays a High Price

Admiral Cunningham was given the responsibility of stopping a seaborne invasion. On the night of 20/21 May two cruiser forces—*Dido, Ajax, Orion* and three destroyers under Rear Admiral Glennie; and *Calcutta, Naiad, Perth, Carlisle* and four destroyers under Rear Admiral King—patrolled the northern approaches to Crete. No invasion forces were encountered and at daylight the two forces withdrew to the south. However, the Luftwaffe soon found them. *Ajax* was damaged with a near miss and in the next attack by Italian high-level bombers, *Juno* was sunk when a bomb exploded in her magazine. The destroyer went down in two minutes with a heavy loss of life.

The night of 21 May proved more fruitful for Cunningham's hunters. Long-range air reconnaissance reported an invasion force between Milos and Suda Bay. Cunningham ordered his admirals to sink the invaders during the night and, if necessary, attack northwards in daylight on the following day.

Admiral Glennie drew first blood. Just after midnight he ran pell-mell into a fleet of twenty-five large caiques and small steamers escorted by the Italian destroyer, *Lupo*, and E boats about seven miles off Suda Bay.

The British cruisers and destroyers switched on searchlights and opened fire with all armament. For two and a half hours the carnage continued. A number of enemy craft were rammed and the battered remnants of this force returned to Milos, with the damaged *Lupo*. The only return fire was from riflemen and machine-gunners on the doomed vessels. As one German soldier of 5th Mountain Division later reported: 'The searchlights appeared like fingers of death'.

Meanwhile, Admiral King's force had met nothing during the night. At dawn King ordered his force to the north. Heavy air attacks developed at 7.00 a.m. but were successfully fought off. At 8.30 a.m. *Perth* sighted a large caique loaded with German troops and promptly sank it. The destroyers then sighted a small steamer which was similarly despatched. At 10.00 a.m. the main armada was sighted. The convoy, 4,000 troops bound for Heraklion under escort of the Italian destroyer, *Sagittario*, had already been ordered to turn back by the German Admiral Schuster.

The Italian destroyer laid a smoke screen, but not before its huge fleet of caiques had been sighted. At this moment, with the enemy at his mercy, Admiral King decided to withdraw. His reason was the ammunition position of his ships and the increasing danger from air attack. The admiral was later to be severely criticised by Cunningham for not attacking and destroying this invasion force and for contributing, with Colonel Andrews, to the loss of Crete. Even at this stage of the battle the German High Command was seriously considering the evacuation of their forces from Crete. Four thousand more dead, on top of an estimate of 5,000 they already had, would have been too much for the High Command to stomach at that stage of the war.

As King's squadron retired it came under heavier air attack. *Naiad* was the first hit. Two turrets were put out of action and her speed fell to 16 knots. *Carlisle*'s turn was next. Her captain was killed and damage was extensive. At 1.30 p.m. the squadron joined Admiral Rawling's battle fleet and *Warspite* was hit by a heavy bomb. Her starboard 4-inch and 6-inch batteries were completed wrecked.

Admiral Glennie's force had also joined the main fleet and the combined force cruised westwards.

Disaster was to follow. *Greyhound*, which had tarried to deal with two caiques, was hit by two bombs as she hurried to rejoin the fleet. *Kandahar* and *Kingston* were detached to take off the crew. To give added cover *Gloucester* and *Fiji*, both low in ammunition, were ordered to stand by. At 3.00 p.m., despite intense bombing and strafing, *Greyhound*'s crew were taken off. The small force turned to rejoin the fleet.

Gloucester was next. Three bombs crashed into her within sight of the fleet and at 3.50 p.m., disabled and burning, she was left to her fate.

Fiji was the unluckiest ship of all. A single Messerschmitt 109 dived out of a cloud and dropped its one bomb beside the cruiser, holing her in the engine room. Half an hour later another bomber found her and sunk her.

The first phase of the naval battle was drawing to a tragic close but one more tragedy remained. The 5th Destroyer Flotilla, under the command of Captain Lord Louis Mountbatten, arrived from Malta on 22 May. Cunningham had ordered his main fleet to return to Alexandria because of a corrupted signal which led him to believe his heavy ships had exhausted their ack-ack ammunition.

Mountbatten was ordered to search for survivors of *Gloucester* and *Fiji* and then patrol the northern approaches. The destroyers *Kelly*, *Kashmir* and *Kipling* enjoyed an eventful night. They sunk two caiques in the entrance to Suda Bay and later stood off Maleme aerodrome and bombarded the German positions. At first light they were steaming south to safety, but at 8.00 a.m. twenty-four dive bombers located them. *Kashmir* went first when struck by a 500-pound bomb. She sank immediately. A few minutes later *Kelly* was hit and capsized while twisting at 30 knots. *Kipling* picked up survivors after surviving hours of unrelenting attacks by bombers.

The price of forestalling a German seaborne invasion was high— too high when the differing figures are dissected. Cunningham reported 4,000 Germans killed in the attempt and added that no seaborne Germans landed during the battle. German official records showed 13 officers and 311 other ranks were lost in the seaborne invasion. One officer and 35 men of 100 Regiment landed on Crete on the night of 21 May. Between 28 and 30 May, the period of the evacuation, some 2,000 men with tanks, artillery and transport were landed by sea at Suda Bay.

British Naval casualties in the engagements of 20–23 May were five times greater than those of the Germans.

I regard both sets of figures as exaggerations. The true figure is possibly an average, say 1,500 to 2,000. Some weeks after the battle ended I was swimming off Suda Bay and swam through several hundred German bodies weighted down with their equipment. At Maleme some days later, two or three hundred more were brought up on the beach. These two spots were fifteen miles apart.

Victory and Defeat

On land a strange torpor had overcome the main forces at Maleme and Heraklion. Although on 20 May they had dealt crushing blows on the invaders, on the 21st they licked their wounds. The New Zealanders at Maleme had fallen back from Hill 107 and in doing so had lost their ability to bring direct fire on the aerodrome. During the day the Germans landed a complete Mountain battalion.

An attack by the Maori Battalion that evening succeeded in reaching the airstrip, but they were not supported and were forced to withdraw with heavy casualties.

Plans for large-scale attacks never eventuated. There was a failure to appreciate the urgent need to stop the German use of the aerodrome. On 22, 23 and 24 May the Germans pushed the New Zealanders back and the Luftwaffe, impotent in the first two days, now attacked the troops continuously.

At Heraklion, after a spirited attack on the first day, the defenders rested on their laurels. The Germans had been driven clear of the airfield but were left almost unmolested.

Only at Retimo, where the defenders were outnumbered and where the battle had been joined with two days' ammunition and food, was the battle fought correctly. At first light on 21 May separate battles were fought on the two hills which flanked the airstrip.

During the night the Germans, under Major Kroh, had built up to a force of 500, supported by mortars and a large number of machine-guns. They attacked up the hills at first light behind a creeping barrage. At the same time a company of 2/1st Battalion was moving down to attack the Germans. The Australians were hit by a barrage and suffered heavy casualties. Lieutenant-Colonel Campbell immediately committed every man of his force and attacked frontally and from the flank. A furious battle developed, which was fought hand to hand. The Germans were caught in a pincer movement and were cut to pieces. Two-thirds of the paratroopers were killed or wounded in the attack. The remainder turned and ran to take refuge in an olive-oil factory at the nearby village of Stavromenos.

On Hill B the fighting had continued through the night. The 2/11th Battalion sought the Germans out, and amongst the prisoners they took was the German commander, Colonel Sturm.

From the beginning of the battle a small force of twenty gunners and others had been cut off on the crown of the hill. Completely surrounded, they armed themselves with captured German weapons and held off the paratroopers throughout the night. At dawn the 2/11th launched a bayonet attack from three sides of the hill. To conserve their ammunition they were told to shoot only in an emergency. It was my experience to watch that bayonet charge from the top of the hill.

The West Australians never hesitated, not even to take prisoners. They drove completely through the German positions. Enemy survivors fled down the hill and made their way to a tiny village called Platanes. When the battles for the hills ended the defenders were confronted by a scene of destruction hard to describe. In an area of three acres lay 400 dead Germans and approximately 100 Australian dead. A thousand or more coloured parachutes festooned the grisly scene and the blackened wrecks of eight or nine burnt out Junkers troop carriers stood out starkly.

The defenders immediately attacked again. At Stavromenos the 100 or so Germans were stiffly entrenched in the fortress-like olive-oil factory. In the opposite direction the enemy had been driven back to the equally strong Church of St George.

General Student's concern for his troops increased with each passing day. On 22 May he sent a Fiesler Stork float plane to contact the survivors at Perivolia. It landed just off the beach and was immediately blown to pieces by Australian gunners. Next day a second float plane landed near Stavromenos. It too was destroyed by the gunners.

General Freyberg threw away another chance of winning the battle on 21 May. When the German attacks on the two hills were defeated at Retimo, two motorised battalions of Australian troops were idly waiting at Georgiopolous, eighteen miles to the east. At Heraklion, thirty miles to the west, Brigadier Chappel had two motorised battalions which could be safely disengaged. These troops could have quickly cleaned up the German remnant at Retimo and the six battalions could have reinforced the New Zealanders at Maleme. However, Freyberg informed Campbell no troops were available.

The Navy endeavoured to land infantry reinforcements on the south coast of the island on 23 May. The infantry landing ship *Glenroy*, escorted by *Coventry* and two sloops, made the attempt. They were turned back by heavy air attacks.

The RAF was ordered to accept any losses to stop the air reinforcements to Maleme. It was an unrealistic order. Air Marshall Longmore lacked the aircraft to make any impression. Several night raids were made on Maleme with little result. Odd sorties were made in daylight with Hurricanes fitted with extra tanks, but their limited range enabled them to remain over Crete for only a few minutes. Six were shot down by our ships.

On the night of 23 May the destoyers *Jaguar* and *Defender* unloaded a small shipment of ammunition at Suda Bay. On this day three German battalions of Mountain troops and a field battery were landed at Maleme and General Student knew he had won the Battle of Crete. His strategy, formulated that day, reflects the importance the battle at Retimo occupied in German minds. The general ordered that the Maleme forces were to fight their way through to Retimo.

At the same time there were serious misgivings in the British Headquarters. The Maleme defenders were being pushed steadily back to Suda Bay, although at Retimo both battalions carried out attacks each day. The olive-oil factory at Stavromenos fell on 26 May. Two 'I' tanks, which had had their sides blown out in Libya, were used in the attack. Some seventy Germans were killed and another sixty taken prisoner. Of the 2,000 Germans landed, 700 to 800 were now dead and 400 were held as prisoners, Colonel Sturm included, while another 200 held a line based on the Church of St George at Perivolia.

On 27 May the 2/11th launched a full-scale attack on the church. The two tanks, now manned by Australians after their original crews had refused to man them, bogged on the side of the road. This attack would have succeeded had not the troops been caught in the open by enemy fighters. Forty were killed by strafing and almost as many wounded.

At dawn on the next morning the attack was repeated. One tank penetrated the defences but its crew were either dead or wounded. The second tank was disabled ten feet from the enemy stronghold. It continued to fire throughout the day and the crew escaped after dark. One company of infantry broke the German line but there was no reserve to exploit the breakthrough. The troops had now been without rations for four days and survived on rations taken from the German dead. Most were using German weapons as their own ammunition was exhausted.

On 28 and 29 May the attacks were renewed but the exhaustion of nine days and nights was telling. The only supplies to reach Retimo arrived on the night of the 26th. This was 1,000 rounds of ammunition and a few cases of bully beef and biscuit. It arrived on an MLB (Motor Landing Barge) commanded by Lieutenant R.A. (Sailor) Haig, who was the Navy's hero in the Battle of Crete. He operated his clumsy vessel throughout the campaign, carrying supplies to Heraklion and bringing tanks from Heraklion to Suda Bay. The barge was concealed in a cave during the day and operated at night. When the evacuation started Haig sailed the craft around to the southern coast and ferried troops to the waiting ships, after which he brought the MLB safely back to Alexandria. Strange to relate, Haig received no recognition.

When Haig left Suda Bay on this last voyage, it was Freyberg's intention that he convey evacuation instructions to Retimo. The officer carrying the instructions was late in arriving and no hint of evacuation reached the Retimo force.

To complete the story of this sector, on 30 May it was noted that the Germans were using field artillery for the first time in the battle. Lieutenant-Colonel Campbell now decided he would unite the two decimated battalions and hold one line on the edge of the airstrip. This was carried out during that night.

At first light next morning the Germans launched a full-scale two-pronged attack. It was led by German tanks, followed by a motorcycle battalion and motorised infantry. Before they were overwhelmed, the Australians hit back again. They poured intense fire into the motorcycle battalion which sustained heavy casualties. As the German tanks and infantry overran the defences the 2/11th Battalion, which was closest to the hills, rallied under their commanding officer, Major

Sandover, and smashed through the German line to the mountains. The majority were captured in the next few weeks but some succeeded in escaping to Egypt. That morning Student informed Hitler the battle was won, to which the Führer sourly replied, 'But at what a price!'

Meanwhile at Maleme the position continued to deteriorate. A battalion of Commandos had been landed on 24 May to reinforce the New Zealanders and Australians, but not once did the defenders launch a large counterattack to destroy the Germans.

The Evacuation

On 26 May, with suggestions of evacuation being made by Freyberg, the Navy launched an air attack on the German air base at Scarpanto. The carrier *Formidable* launched eight aircraft for the attack. Results were negligible and in the action the carrier was heavily damaged, the destroyer *Nubian* disabled and the battleship *Barham* hit.

The decision to evacuate Crete was reached on the following day. Ironically, it coincided with an order from Hitler to General Lohr to withdraw the bulk of Air Fleet IV to Germany for the attack on Russia. By 28 May the first day of the evacuation, German air strength was drastically reduced. This information was known by Cunningham through his excellent intelligence within hours and could well have altered the evacuation decision, but it was not seized upon.

The Navy was now to face disaster again. Heraklion was evacuated on the night of the 28th, without the loss of a single man. The evacuation fleet, *Orion*, *Ajax*, *Dido* and six destroyers, was commanded by Rear Admiral Rawlings.

Ajax was near-missed before it reached Crete and an inaccurate damage report caused her to return to Alexandria. *Imperial* was also near-missed. The remaining ships embarked the troops efficiently. At 3.20 a.m. on 29 May the ships began the return voyage. Minutes later, *Imperial* lost control, her steering gear having been damaged by the near-miss. *Hotspur* was detached to take off *Imperial*'s troops and crew and the damaged destroyer was sunk.

Hereward's turn came next. She was hit when waves of Stukas attacked. Her speed fell off and she was left to her fate. Dive-bombers later sunk her off the coast of Crete. *Decoy* was near-missed shortly afterwards and her speed fell to 21 knots, while *Orion* sustained damage from a near miss in the same attack. This was followed by a strafing attack in which Captain Back was killed.

Dido was hit by a large bomb on B turret at 8.15 a.m. Three-quarters of an hour later *Orion* sustained a hit which destroyed A turret, and at 10.45 she was hit again. A large bomb crashed down into the mess decks, killing 280. *Orion* finally arrived at Alexandria under tow. Her story has been told by Ron Atwill in *Naval Historical Review*, 1971.

The first evacuation had been a calamity.

Meanwhile, the troops had been streaming across the island from Suda Bay to Sfakia. The rearguards were not hard pressed. Student had sent the main force to relieve his Retimo troops and two battalions of Mountain Troops were given the task of harassing the evacuation.

On the night of 28 May the destroyers *Napier*, *Nizam*, *Kelvin* and *Kandahar* evacuated 1,100 troops. A stronger fleet arrived on the following night, consisting of *Phoebe*, *Perth*, *Glengyle*, *Calcutta*, *Coventry*, *Jarvis*, *Janus* and *Hasty*. Six thousand troops were lifted. The cost was *Calcutta* sunk and *Perth* damaged.

A smaller fleet arrived off Sfakia on the 30th. It was *Napier* and *Nizam*. *Kandahar* had broken down on passage and *Kelvin* returned to Alexandria with bomb damage. The two Australian ships took off 1,400. Next night *Phoebe*, *Kimberley*, *Hotspur*, *Jackal* and the fast mine-layer *Abdiel* took off another 6,000 troops.

This was the end. Cunningham informed Churchill that he could not risk his remaining ships. The Battle of Crete was over. Some 9,000 troops were left to be taken prisoner.

The Cost

The cost of the battle was heavy. The British Army forces lost 1,742 dead, 1,737 wounded and 11,835 prisoners. To this may be added 800 killed, wounded or captured in the Heraklion convoy. The Navy casualties were 1,828 killed and 183 wounded. The German casualties were 4,500 dead, and no figure was given for wounded. To this figure must be added 327 killed in the sea invasion. One hundred and seventy Junkers transports were lost, along with sixty-four other aircraft (these are German figures).

The Airborne Army never recovered. The Storm Regiment alone lost 50 officers and 1,000 men killed. On the first day of the battle the Germans lost more men than they had in the first nineteen months of the war. Furthermore, many of these were the cream of German youth, highly trained athletes who had volunteered for the campaign.

The postscript to the Cretan campaign, from the German point of view, was written in 1942. When the capture of Malta was mooted, Hitler refused another airborne operation, noting 'The cost of Crete was too high'.

However, the greatest loss of the campaign was that suffered by the Royal Navy. They damaged one destroyer and sank perhaps twenty caiques and small steamers, but at a cost of four cruisers and six destroyers sunk, and three battleships, one aircraft carrier, six cruisers, one landing ship and eight destroyers damaged.

So ended the land and sea battle for Crete, according to the book. Indeed it did not end until May 1945. A strong resistance movement tied down five German divisions, a considerable air force and a small navy right up to the surrender.

The British War Cemetery at Suda Bay.

The German War Memorial near Maleme.

A memorial service at the Australian war memorial at
Stavromenos in 1979. The memorial was erected by the Cretans
of Retimo. Drawings for the relief casting on the stele were made
by Lew Lind.

"My father fought the German invaders when they fell on this
farm in 1941. He was driven back into the hills but when the
Australians hurled the invaders back to the sea with their blood-
anointed bayonets, he returned. When he died I was proud to
honour his wishes—one-fifth of my inheritance was to be given
as a memorial to the Australians who fought and died here.
Their memory will live forever."

Stelios Zacariadakis,
Consecration of the Australian Memorial,
Stavromenos near Rethymnon, 1972

The author with the Pandelakis brothers at the village of Fratti in 1985.

The author with monks at Preveli Monastery in 1985. The two plaques in the background record the monastery's part in the submarine evacuations in 1941.

Mythros revisited. Lew Lind (wearing hat) with Andreas, Mike Munro of Australia's '60 Minutes' television program and Marcos Dimitakakis. The house in the background sheltered the author in 1941.

The bond which has existed between Australians and Cretans for more than half a century is a bond of blood forged on the battlefields of the rugged island in 1941 and in the mountainous interior during the bitter years of the German occupation.

No man had done more to foster this unique relationship between one of the youngest nations of the world and one of the oldest than Marcos Polioudakis of Rethymnon, Crete. As a young schoolboy in 1941 Marcos Polioudakis saw his father and other relatives executed by the Germans for succouring wounded Australian soldiers. He also saw and admired the Australians defending Rethymnon who, despite being outnumbered and having inferior arms, defeated the cream of the German Army before being overwhelmed by superior German forces after the Allies had evacuated the western end of the island.

Marcos Polioudakis was the originator of the plan to erect a memorial to the Australians on the hillside where the Australians achieved their first victory over the German invader at Rethymnon. When the Zacariadakis family of Stavromenos donated a section of land for this purpose he contributed to and encouraged others to contribute to enable the full area of the memorial to be purchased and the memorial to be built.

In the 1960s he cultivated new communication with the Australian veterans. In 1972 it was his honour to welcome the Prime Minister of Australia, the Honourable Gough Whitlam and Mrs Whitlam, to Stavromenos. Three years later he hosted the first reunion of Australian veterans at Rethymnon. His home and hospitality has been available to all veterans and their families for more than thirty years.

Marcos Polioudakis was the key organiser for the visit of Australian veterans to Rethymnon during the 50th Anniversary Tour of the Battles of Greece and Crete.

His services for promoting this unique Australian-Cretan relationship were recognised by the Australian Government in 1988 when he became the first citizen of Crete to be awarded the Medal of the Order of Australia. The investiture was made by the Governor General of Australia, Sir Ninian Stephens.

Mr Marcos Polioudakis *(right)* and the author at a memorial service in Rethymnon in 1990.

NOTES

Chapter 1: Isle of Doom

1. HMS *Ajax*, cruiser: 6,985 tons, 522 feet long, 55.5 foot beam, eight 6-inch and eight 4-inch guns. Built by Vickers Armstrong, Barrow, 1934. Sold out of service, November 1949, and broken up by Cashmore, Newport.

2. An unknown Australian soldier poet epitomised the feelings of us all in those days:

> Here we sit on the Isle of Crete,
> Bludging on our blistered feet.
> We sailed to Greece to win the war,
> We marched and groaned beneath our load,
> Whilst Jerry bombed us off the road,
> He chased us here he chased us there;
> The bastards chased us everywhere.
> And whilst he dropped his load of death,
> We cursed the bloody RAF.
> Yes the RAF was there in force,
> They left a few at home of course.
> We saw the entire force one day,
> When a Hurricane went the other way;
> And when we heard the wireless news,
> When portly Winston aired his views—
> The RAF are now in Greece
> Fighting hard to win the peace;
> We scratched our heads and said, 'pig's arse',
> For this to us was just a farce,
> For if in Greece the airforce be—
> Then where the bloody hell are we?
> The bullets whizzed, the big guns roared,
> We bawled for ships to get aboard;
> At last they came and on we got,
> And sailed away from that cursed spot.
> Then the navy landed us in Crete,
> The bloody army marched us off our bloody feet.
> The food was light, the water crook—
> I got fed up and slung my hook.
> And now it looks like even betting,

A man will soon become a Cretan;
And spend his days in blackest gloom—
On Adolph Hitler's Isle of Doom.

3. The heavy cruiser HMS *York* had been sunk with the tanker *Pericles* in Suda Bay on 26 March by Italian explosive motor boats.

4. The guns were without sights and instruments and the ammunition was unreliable. Sighting was done by peering through the barrel. However, they were still to inflict damage on the enemy in the battle.

5. The barge was an A-lighter, a forerunner of the Landing Craft Infantry. It made a second run to Retimo on the night of 26–27 May with ammunition and stores. The commanding officer was Lieutenant R.A. (Sailor) Haig, Royal Navy.

6. Several pilots were American volunteers who had enlisted in the Lone Eagle Squadron.

7. Major R.L. Sandover, commanding the 2/11th Battalion, who was fluent in German, and Lieutenant-Colonel I. Campbell interpreted the notations on the maps.

8. That is, 2/11th Battalion.

9. We had no small arms in the section to defend ourselves. Our only weapons were a shovel and a pick.

10. Captain J. Fitzhardinge.

11. This was a captured German weapon.

12. Captain G.W. Mann.

13. Colonel Sturm, Commander of the German force at Retimo.

14. 2/1st Battalion.

15. The field hospital was later overrun by 2/11th Battalion and was amalgamated with the Australian field hospital.

16. 2/1st Battalion.

17. Sargeant J. Millar.

18. Lieutenant D. Wells.

19. The German-occupied village was Adhele.

20. The village of Platanes.

21. The steeple was never rebuilt and the base where it was shorn off may be seen today.

Chapter 2: Beginning of the End

1. 2/11th Battalion.

2. Since 23 May the Australian and German casualty clearing stations had operated as one in the valley below the village of Pigi. The Australian medical officers were Captains A.G. Carter (2/1st

Battalion) and J.J. Ryan (2/11th Battalion). With their German
equivalents, they were treating 147 Australian, 51 Greek and 252
German wounded. These figures escalated as the battle progressed.
3. 2/1st Battalion.

Chapter 3: Tank Fiasco

1. The tanks were British 'I' tanks which had been salvaged after
being knocked out by the Italians in Libya. Both were in poor
mechanical order and repairs had been superficial.
2. Battle statistics were as follows:

Ground strength

Australians	1,400	(not fully armed)
Greeks	2,000	(largely untrained)
Germans	2,000	(reinforced on 28 May by 2,000 fresh troops from Suda Bay)

Air strength

Australian	Restricted to two raids by bombers
Greek	Nil
German	Continuous cover by fighters, dive-bombers and bombers

Casualties

Australian	133 killed, 230 wounded, 1,200 prisoners of war
Greek	Not known
German	630 killed, 700 wounded, 550 prisoners of war later released.

Chapter 4: Surrender

1. Lieutenant-Colonel Ian Campbell, who commanded the Battle of
Retimo.
2. Our persecutors were support troops landed in the last days of the
battle at Suda Bay. The paratroopers against whom we fought
generally treated us fairly.
3. This was to cause us the torment of diarrhoea.

Chapter 5: Battle Aftermath

1. A macabre aspect of this swim was the number of bodies of fully
equipped German soldiers we saw on the seabed off this beach. We
were later to learn that these were the casualties from the large convoy

of enemy caiques sunk by ships of the Royal Navy in the first days of the battle.

2. The village of Pirgos, east of Maleme.

3. Much of the destruction had been wrought by guns of B Troop of my regiment, 2/3rd Field Regiment.

4. We were later to learn this was not strictly correct and that the airfield had been lost through bungling at the highest level of command. The loss of Maleme resulted in the loss of Crete.

5. One interesting item unloaded was three sacks of Iron Crosses which several days later we were to witness being presented to surviving parachutists by General Student, who commanded the German airborne forces.

6. This was in fact an irrigation canal which served surrounding farms and vineyards. It was five feet deep by fifteen feet wide and concrete-lined. At the time it carried about eighteen inches of filthy water. The canal, which was topped by a barbed-wire fence, formed the southern boundary of the prisoner-of-war camp.

7. The young paratroopers' love of singing later worked to my advantage. Two German soldiers asked me to teach them the words and tunes of some of our modern songs. I spent two very pleasant days on this chore, which was a welcome relief from the labour gangs. My students did not realise I sang out of tune and that I substituted words which were not very complimentary to their nationality.

8. Our original captors, parachutists and Austrian Mountain troops, had been replaced by garrison troops who lacked the respect of the fighting troops.

Chapter 6: An Idea is Born

1. We had very little contact with the Cretan population before and during the battle and consequently did not know where their loyalty lay.

2. Gunner Farleigh (Flap) James of New South Wales and Gunner Frederick Sharp of Western Australia. Fred Sharp was recaptured in 1942 and was later a prisoner of war in Germany. Flap James eluded capture and was evacuated from Crete in 1943.

3. Bombadier H. (Bluey) Armstrong of New South Wales. He was recaptured with Fred Sharp in 1942.

4. The large village of Voukolies on the road from Maleme to Paleochora on the south coast.

Chapter 7: Among Friends

1. Crete in the summer months is a veritable garden. Some 1,200 varieties of European flowers are native to the island.
2. A small village to the east of Voukolies, probably Lakia.
3. The meeting place selected was the fishing village of Souya on the south coast. I chose it at random from the page of a school atlas I had found at Maleme.
4. This nocturnal trek had taken us through the villages of Paleo Roumita and Nea Roumita and across the high spine of the White Mountains. In the morning we stopped at a village which my guide called Spina.
5. I believe this was the village of Anisaraki, south of the large centre of Rodovani.
6. Moni, a famous resistance village which was burnt and had many of its people executed by the Germans in 1943. (Many British escapees met with a rebuff here due to pronouncing it as 'Mooni', a sensitive part of a woman's anatomy.)
7. The fiery Cretan spirit rakki.

Chapter 8: To Seize a Boat

1. The small fishing village of Souya is on the south coast of western Crete. It is flanked on both the east and west by rough mountain country. The village was under the surveillance of German troops for most of the occupation.
2. Gunner Dick Plant of New South Wales served with the 2/3rd Light Anti-Aircraft Regiment in Crete. He fully recovered from the illness which was later confirmed as pneumonia and yellow jaundice. Zebrou was too small to hide a British soldier for a long period and after a month Dick moved to the larger village of Temenia, where he was cared for by the Daskalaki family. He remained free until early 1942, when he was recaptured in the large German drive through western Crete.
3. Gregori Zorbazakis was the head of the village of Zebrou. As a young man he worked in the United States where he acquired fluency in English. On his return he married and settled on his ancestral farm. His sons were Nicko, Adoni and Manoli. All four served in the resistance movement.
4. Zebrou is one of the smallest villages in Crete and is not shown on the map. It still consists of only four small whitewashed houses

and a few outhouses. Soon after Dick Plant left the Germans heard we had been sheltered in the village and they burned the Zorbazakis house. It was later rebuilt but remained under suspicion until the Germans left Crete.

5. The treatment performed on Dick Plant is called cupping and was the only treatment for pneumonia in eighteenth- and nineteenth-century Europe. Folk medicine was widely practised amongst Cretans, whose herbal treatments were extensive. They performed a number of operations on British soldiers during the occupation, including the successful removal of a bullet lodged near the kidney of a New Zealand soldier. This operation was performed with a knife without any medication and the soldier lived.

6. The village was Koustogerako (we called it Costa Jericho) and it had been the centre of resistance against foreign invaders for more than five centuries. Andartes from this rugged area had fought oppressors from Byzantine, Venice and Turkey and were now fighting the Germans. Built high on a 2,000 foot conical peak and with a population of about 240, it surveyed the Selino valley. Together with its sister villages of Moni and Livades it was burnt by the Germans in 1943 and many of its people were executed. The Koustogerako fighters took savage reprisals on the Germans. The village has since been rebuilt. The holocaust is remembered in a patriotic Cretan folk song: 'It is thundering in Selino, it is raining, but it is raining bullets. The Germans invaded the three villages. They burned Moni, and Koustogerako and Livades. . .'

Chapter 9: My Strange Captors

1. Spinach grass—an edible native grass.

2. Foremost in this group were the famous resistance family, the Pasterakis, Costas, Georgie, Adonis, Manolie and Vardis all led groups against the German oppressors. Manolie was the guide who led Captain Patrick Leigh Fermor's party in the famous capture and abduction of the German Commander of Crete, General Kriepe, in 1944. A book and a film were later made of this daring exploit, both entitled *Ill Met By Moonlight*. Other prominent families were the Vernadakis, Kosmadakis, Manoudakis and Kandanoleon.

3. From July 1941, English-speaking Germans posing as escapees were infiltrated into the mountain areas of western Crete to locate the hide-outs of British escapees and evaders. This ploy was not successful and was discontinued after a number of agents disappeared.

4. Behind Koustogerako, to the east, is a wilderness of rugged mountain slopes which rise to 7,000 feet. This barren high country desert is uninhabited and is the last refuge of the Cretan agrimi (ibex). It is split to the east by the wild and precipitous Gorge of Samaria and to the north over the spine of the White Mountains by the Omalos. In the spring and summer shepherds move their flocks into this high country, but in the winter it is covered in snow.

5. The village was Samaria, on the western escarpment of the gorge. This remote village was occupied only in the summer and at that time was home to bandits. After leaving Samaria I was fired on by hidden marksmen.

6. I was looking down on the fertile valley of Omalos. It is a circular-shaped basin with a level floor. Before the battle commenced the British High Command gave serious through to building an airfield in this valley and that of Lasithi in eastern Crete. Both valleys, because of their rich soil, are regarded as the bread baskets of the island. Because of its proximity to the White Mountains, the Germans maintained a strong garrison at Laki.

7. This was in the tiny village of Zourva above Meskala, which is overlooked by the frowning heights of Lefka Ori.

Chapter 10: In Good Company

1. Some 20,000 Cretans between eighteen and thirty years of age served in the 5th Cretan Division which fought the Italians in Albania. When the Greek Army surrendered in April 1941, many Cretans stole caiques and crossed to Crete. This accounted for the absence of men of military age in the villages.

2. By this time it was difficult to distinguish me from the Cretan youths with whom I travelled through the mountains. Piece by piece my uniform was replaced by Cretan clothing and, to add to the deception, many of the villagers were wearing items of discarded British uniforms. The greatest problem initially was my tan Australian boots, but after many weeks they fell to pieces from walking over the rough terrain. I discarded them and later wore old Cretan boots or sometimes went barefooted. My hair was long and uncut and the lack of a razor resulted in a fuzz of beard. Months of living in the open under the burning sun scorched my skin to a deep brown. After this first confrontation with German soldiers I gained confidence and was never again alarmed by these chance meetings.

3. Dimifrouliana is the only true lake in Crete. It lies three miles south-

east of the fishing port of Georgiopolous. At this period it was one of the worst areas in the island for European malaria.

Chapter 11: Up a Tree

1. Towards the end of June 1941, the Germans offered rewards up to 10,000 drachma for information leading to the apprehension of British escapees and evaders. There was little response and in the months which followed the reward was increased.

At the same time thousands of poorly printed leaflets encouraging the British to surrender were distributed in villages and dropped from the air:

Soldiers of the British Army, Air Force and Royal Navy—
There are many of you still hiding in the mountains, valleys and villages.
You have to present yourself at once to the German troops.
Every attempt to flee will be in vain.
Every opposition will be completely useless!
The coming winter will force you to leave the mountains.
Only soldiers who present themselves at once will be sure of soldierly captivity of war. On the contrary, who is met in civil clothes will be treated as a spy.

The Commander of Crete

This poorly worded leaflet met with little response.

2. The Cretans rolled the leaf and smoked it but we cut it fine and wrapped it in paper. Either way, it tasted foul and smelt worse.

3. Patima, a small mountain hamlet of ten or twelve houses, east of Kournas.

4. This was the village of Koufi, three miles east of the large centre of Episkopi.

5. Since leaving Koustogerako I had directed my steps back to Retimo where I had been captured. This decision took me out of western Crete where the majority of British troops were located. Of the 300 soldiers still at large, some 250 were in the western half of the island hemmed in by the inhospitable heights of the White Mountains. Each step now took me into an area comparatively free of other escapees.

Chapter 12: A Circle is Closed

1. I approached the city from the south, descending the high escarpment which forms a dramatic background to the old Venetian

port. German soldiers were visible in the streets so I kept to the city outskirts.

2. Gunner Ian McNeilage of South Australia.

3. The roadblock was between the villages of Platenes and Adhele, about five miles east of Retimo. The bamboo groves which aided my escape still grow beside the road.

4. The Germans initially established cemeteries on the various battlefields in Crete, but in 1973 they were brought together on a hill behind Maleme. The British War Cemetery is at Suda Bay.

5. The road to the south crossed the island to Aghios Galini and Timbaki.

6. This was the village of Mythros, some twelve miles by road and track from Retimo.

7. It was the grape-harvesting season and throughout Crete the grapes hung in huge purple bunches under the vines.

Chapter 13: Priest with a Gun

1. The priest was Lieutenant-Commander Francis G. Pool, Royal Navy, an intelligence officer who had been landed by a submarine at Limni on the south coast of Crete on the night of July 17. Limni was five miles from the Holy Monastery of St John, which looked out to sea from a bluff headland. Pool's contact was the Most Reverend

The Holy Monastery of St John at Preveli. In July 1941 it served as a transit depot for escaped prisoners of war.

Agathangolos Lagouvardos, abbot of the monastery and the most important figure of the Greek Orthodox Church in Crete.

The elderly abbot used his influence to muster patriotic Cretans and resistance groups to gather the British evaders and escapees at the monastery for eventual evacuation to Egypt. The monastery soon became a transit depot and attracted the attention of the Germans.

Unfortunately, the majority of the estimated 300 British still at large were at the far western end of the island and the path to Preveli was over the precipitous spine of the White Mountains. The journey was considered impossible without guides.

The first group of sixty-five was gathered at Preveli within ten days and embarked in the submarine HMS *Thrasher* at Limni. They arrived at Alexandria on 31 July.

Shortly after the submarine's departure from Limni a strong German force swooped on the monastery. Local Cretans warned the monks of the approaching force and the British soldiers still remaining and Abbot Lagouvardos were spirited away to friendly villages before the raid.

Many of the monastery's seventy monks were arrested and imprisoned and the monastery was ransacked. The Germans removed many precious relics from the historic building.

An extensive search was made for the abbot, who successfully eluded the searchers and was taken to Alexandria in a caique commanded by Lieutenant G.J. Greenway of the Australian 2/11th Battalion. Abbot Lagouvardos died in Egypt in 1942.

Commander Pool organised new holding areas for the escapees in the high villages on the eastern side of the Kourtaliotiko Gorge, and there was to be one more British submarine from Limni before the Germans established a strong garrison in the area.

Commander Pool was truly the mystery man of Crete. Research by a number of investigators has uncovered little of his background. One story, like many others which remain unconfirmed, is that Pool entered the Royal Naval College in the early 1930s and on graduation opted for intelligence. The same source believes he later received religious training in the Greek Orthodox Church at the Mount Athos Monastery in Northern Greece. He is recorded as being the manager of Imperial Airways at Heraklion in 1938. A blank exists in his activities between late 1941 and December 1944. One source claims he was murdered in Athens in December 1944, when attending peace talks between Royalists and members of ELAS. However, former resistance fighter and author, George Psychoundakis, states in his book *The Cretan Runner*: 'Commander F.G. Pool, D.S.O., D.S.C., Royal Navy, died in Athens in 1947'.

Fifty years after my first meeting with him at the village of Mythros, Pool remains an enigma.

2. Andreas and his cousin Marcos Dimitrakakis, the former in his early twenties and the latter aged eighteen, were Commander Pool's runners at this time. Andreas lived in Mythros and Marcos in Selli. Despite their close association with the intelligence officer, they knew little of his background. Today, Marcos operates a tourist hotel in Retimo and Andreas is a farmer in Mythros.

3. This was Selli the village of iron gates, almost every house had one. It was a prosperous village and there was no shortage of food.

4. Cretan customs at this time were almost biblical. It was quite common on arriving at a Cretan home for the lady of the house to remove one's shoes and socks and bathe one's feet in warm water and olive oil. No matter how poor the home, few visitors departed without bread and cheese wrapped in a clean linen cloth. The best blanket in the house was reserved for the use of a guest. When one left a village the women crossed themselves and offered a prayer for the safety of the visitor.

5. During the warm summer evenings the flat roofs of the Cretan houses became the forums of the villages. The men gathered here with their krassi and rakki to talk to the early hours of the morning.

6. Every village in the mountains had its armoury. The firearms ranged from Turkish flintlocks to British Lee-Enfields and German Mausers.

7. A highlight of this farewell feast was a demonstration of Cretan dancing. The dancers were men, the women of Crete having vowed not to dance or to wear any colour other than black until Greece was free again.

8. The humble snail was an important item on the Cretan menu. During the severe winter of 1942 the appearance of plagues of snails saved many villages from certain starvation. This providential occurrence is still called The Miracle of the Snails.

Chapter 14: Fugitives Foregather

1. This was Fratti, a village of thirty houses perched on a crag above the fearsome Kourtaliotiko Gorge which led down to Limni. In 1942 a British Blenheim bomber crashed nearby and a memorial to the crew was erected in the square.

2. The head of the village was known to us as 'The Fat Man of Fratti' because of great girth. He spoke fluent English and it was said he served in the Royal Navy many years before. He was a close friend of Commander Pool. The Pandelakis family of this village was one of the number who provided guides and fed escapees.

3. The Germans had already raided the nearby Preveli Monastery and arrested many of the monks. Informers had reported the last visit of a British submarine to the coast.

Chapter 15: 'We Move Tonight'

1. British Commandos, known as Layforce, were landed in Crete during the last days of the battle.

2. This was the fabled Bay of Limni, our gateway to escape and freedom. Limni is said to be the fair haven of the Bible where the Apostle Paul wintered on his voyage to Rome. A cave at the base of the eastern headland is said to have contained the Apostle's altar where the first Cretan convert to Christianity and the patron saint of the island, Titus, was baptised. HMS *Merlin*, a survey sloop, claimed to have identified the site in 1853, also noting the suitability of the bay for clandestine operations. (I was to wait forty-nine years before I saw Limni in daylight.)

3. Clothing was in such short supply in Crete that all who left the island during the occupation were required to depart in the nude.

4. All British submarines engaged in this type of operation carried a Royal Marine swimmer. (I renewed my acquaintance with this swimmer in 1986.)

5. Five or six Cretans, who were not included in the party to be evacuated, swam out from the shore and attempted to board the submarine. They were turned back.

6. HMS *Torbay*, 'T' Class submarine: 1,090 tons, 265 feet long, 26.5 feet beam, one 4-inch gun and eleven torpedo tubes. Built at Chatham Dockyard, 1940. Sold out of service and broken up by Ward, Briton Ferry 12/1945.

A 'T' class submarine similar to HMS *Torbay*.

7. Crete regained its freedom on 23 May 1945, four years, less one week, after it fell under the heel of Germany. The island was surrendered to the British who had lost it.

8. We were bathed, shaved and shorn of our locks by the crew of the depot ship. Outfitted in British Army uniform we were whisked to the Citadel in Cairo to undergo ten days of interrogation by intelligence officers. After a fortnight we were returned to our units, in my case to Palestine.

INDEX

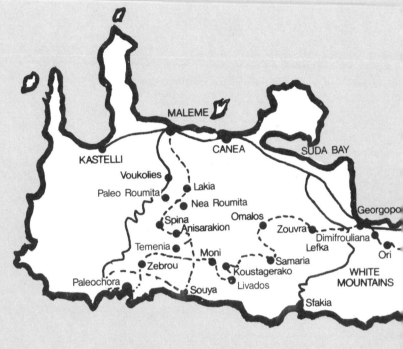

MALEME

CANEA

SUDA BAY

KASTELLI

Voukolies

Lakia

Paleo Roumita

Nea Roumita

Spina

Omalos

Zouvra

Georgopo

Anisarakion

Dimifrouliana

Lefka

Temenia

Moni

Ori

Samaria

Zebrou

Koustagerako

WHITE

Paleochora

Livados

MOUNTAINS

Souya

Sfakia

N

W ——+—— E

S

SCALE : 722,000

KEY

- - - The escape route

—— Roads